Radical Empathy in Multicultural Women's Fiction

Radical Empathy in Multicultural Women's Fiction

From the Library to Liberation

Lara S. Narcisi

LEXINGTON BOOKS
Lanham • Boulder • New York • London

Published by Lexington Books
An imprint of The Rowman & Littlefield Publishing Group, Inc.
4501 Forbes Boulevard, Suite 200, Lanham, Maryland 20706
www.rowman.com

86-90 Paul Street, London EC2A 4NE

British Library Cataloguing in Publication Information Available

Library of Congress Cataloging-in-Publication Data
Names: Narcisi, Lara S., 1975- author.
   Title: Radical empathy in multicultural women's fiction : from the library
      to liberation / Lara S. Narcisi.
   Description: Lanham : Lexington Books, [2023] | Includes bibliographical
      references and index.
   Identifiers: LCCN 2023019196 (print) | LCCN 2023019197 (ebook) | ISBN
      9781666921502 (cloth) | ISBN 9781666921519 (epub)   Subjects: LCSH:
   American fiction--Women authors--History and criticism. |
      American fiction--Minority authors--History and criticism. | Empathy in
      literature. | Minorities in literature. | LCGFT: Literary criticism.
   Classification: LCC PS374.W6 N37 2023 (print) | LCC PS374.W6 (ebook) |
      DDC 813.009/9287--dc23/eng/20230616
   LC record available at https://lccn.loc.gov/2023019196
   LC ebook record available at https://lccn.loc.gov/2023019197

To my mother, who gave me life and language.
To my husband, who saved my life once and makes it worth living every day.

Contents

A Personal Preface

I was born from a book. My parents named me Lara after the romantic heroine of Pasternak's Dr. Zhivago, doomed and damned, but passionate and kind. My mother and I wrote limericks for each other, and my father read to me every night, from *Charlotte's Web* and *Anne of Green Gables,* all the way up to Tolstoy and Kafka. I read while I walk; I bleary-eyed read into dreams and dream through my readings.

I was then, and am now, a curious one, in the dual sense of both odd and avid. I did, I do, choose reading over nearly any other activity. I was, I am, moved near to tears by the scent of pages in a second-hand bookstore, by the textured feel of a soft matte cover beneath my fingers. Books simultaneously sated and stoked my inveterate wanderlust, so my travels are always wrapped in the words of authors: Joyce and Beckett in Ireland; Mishima and Murakami in Japan; Mafouz in Egypt; Llosa in Peru; and Carey in Australia. Rushdie and Lahiri will indubitably rattle the cages of my imagination until I see the India they etched on its walls.

Yet reading retains a reputation as a solitary endeavor, a lonely occupation for introverts. While book clubs and English classes may provide opportunities for communal literary discussion, the reading process itself is still one we think we do alone. I contend, however, that in reading we are always in dialogue with books; who hasn't shouted a warning to a beloved character about to make an unwise decision, or cheered another on for choosing the preferable path? Writers, as readers themselves, are constantly conversing with the texts they have read throughout their lives; they are always absorbing and transforming in the process.

Across time, across countries, I have worked to forge a conversation between the writers of past and present. I have sought connections between works because I believe that fiction creates a dialogue nothing else can; it can create empathy anywhere and everywhere. And if fiction can make us care more and more deeply about others, it can also spur us to action towards social justice. Certain books are parts of conversations between authors that are so loud we can only benefit from listening and joining in ourselves. That is what I hope this book can help us do.

Introduction

Maxine Hong Kingston wanted to know why I didn't think she was funny.

Or at least, that was how I read it. A few decades ago, my very first academic article had been published in *Connotations,* a rather unique journal that sought author's responses to the critical essays discussing their works. Academia doesn't tend to view criticism as a conversation, but rather as a monologue, or occasionally a shouting match. But here was an author writing back to me writing back to her book, *Tripmaster Monkey.* Kingston's reply was gracious and engaging, concluding, "It's good to hear you laugh at the relationship between Zeppelin and Wittman. But you are so serious about the rest of the book. Am I not funny throughout?" ("Response" 179).

Of course she is; the main character is named Wittman Ah Sing, a delightful literary pun, and *Tripmaster Monkey* is a joyful trip all along the way. But it is also a book to take very seriously. I found it by chance in a bookstore while visiting Northern California; literally judging a book by its cover, I was drawn to its pleasing texture, its gold embossing, and its depiction of the Golden Gate bridge on its cover ("here is the bridge, and here am I!," thought I). At the heart of that book is genuine personal transformation: a protagonist who, through art and community, morphs into a better version of himself. Picking up this book at random, in turn, changed me; perhaps it was not a coincidence that the topic of that first article was self-revision.

Kingston agreed with my interpretation, responding: "Though Monkey's motto is 'Be–e–en!'—'Change!'—his transformation was hard won. I'm glad that you saw that he did change, and that his changes are natural, and came about through language. I mean to help build the American language" (179). Of course she did. The wild, playful, complicated free indirect discourse Kingston uses in that novel is, indeed, transformative in its own right. Within the text, the giant communal play Wittman collaboratively creates remakes him in turn, and in the end, he forsakes a literary tradition of war and embraces pacifism. He becomes more community-minded through a communal language, one that evolves through the words he writes, the ones others improvise, and the dialogue created in the process.

Kingston ends her response to my article with two words. After appreciating my interpretation, and gently mocking my solemnity, she concludes: "We communicated." This is what literature can and should do: create moments of both agreement and disagreement, allowing a conversation to develop. When we view reading as a solitary affair, or when we read only literature that mirrors our own ideas and beliefs, we sever ourselves from the communal aspect literature can create. We then lose a fundamental opportunity to develop as scholars, citizens, and activists. Both Wittman's play and the exchange between his author and myself became models for me of what collaborative reading could and should achieve.

This book attempts to create such conversations between women writers of color. As elaborated below, this work is essential to avoid the "single story" narrative perpetuated by studying writers in isolation, or by using a single writer of any given background as a representative for all. Each chapter therefore focuses on two American women writers of color, the first now an established "classic" author of one or more curricular mainstays, and the second of the next generation with an acclaimed book released in the past five years (as of this writing). I selected the author pairings using three criteria: first, the authors share an ethnic heritage (Chinese American, African American, and Chicana, respectively), demonstrating that the canonized author is not the only voice speaking for all women of her ethnicity. Second, in each there is a direct chain of influence; that is to say, the newer writer publicly credits the more established writer as an inspiration, so in a sense the conversation has already begun. Third, in each case the writers explore topics that engage their multiple subject positions, including race, gender, and class. These intersectional topics include, in order: the gender-based silencing of Asian American characters; Black masculinity as seen through journeys into the slavery-stained past; and Chicanas coming of age while negotiating class struggles. The final chapter expands each topic to writers from different previous chapters, modeling the way we can read across cultures as well as within them.

I intend for this process to forge multiple conversations and to suggest the potential for many more. The choice of chapter topics attempts to validate how each author's multiple subject positions of race, gender, class, and so forth are not isolated or discrete categories but uniquely interlocked and mutually impactful, as discussed below. Furthermore, the chapters are not limited to the two principal novelists but also incorporate other relevant and influential writers and texts along the way. This step is crucial, as it brings the dialogue we could create between two writers into a larger conversation: a polylogue, perhaps. The chapter topics, similarly, focus on identity as connected, not separate from, society as a whole, and as such they expand and complicate along the way. For example, gender dynamics often necessitate a discussion of sexuality, or they may change according to one's class position; typically, they will all be impacted by and participate in a culture of patriarchy. At all points, I invite readers to bring their own additional readings and responses into the conversation as well.

Before delving into these specific connections between the authors, chapter one lays the groundwork through an overview of earlier critics and theorists and by providing brief examples of the central importance of fiction, empathy, diversity, and action. This chapter defines and promotes "radical empathy" in fiction, analyzing the ways our reading of novels can create an understanding of the experiences of others that no other medium can achieve, and instigating a change in mindset that can lead to activism. It discusses the importance of both intertextuality and intersectionality as methods of countering the "danger of a single story," as Chimamanda Adichie defines it (*TED*). Exploring complex intersections of both texts and identity positions can enable readers to see outside the individual viewpoint limited by any singular consciousness. This method illuminates how each of these writers is indebted to one another and to others in turn, for, as Virginia Woolf writes in *A Room of One's Own*, "masterpieces are not single or solitary births; they are the outpouring of many years of thinking in common" (65). When we read these authors together, we gain a more complete understanding of this body of literature than we can by reading any of the works in isolation. Empathy for fictional characters has led to social action in the past, as I discuss, and focusing on the shared justice concerns of these authors will, I hope, inspire readers to engage in and expand such activism in the future.

The second chapter demonstrates the process outlined in the introduction by analyzing the way Celeste Ng's 2014 novel, *Everything I Never Told You*, broadens and complicates Maxine Hong Kingston's sense of gendered silence as depicted in her 1976 memoir, *Woman Warrior*. The works have several obvious points of comparison: both begin with a drowned woman who cannot speak for herself, and both subsequently trace her family's desperate attempts to undo the silencing that led to her demise. This chapter builds off the work of Adrienne Rich, who states that private acts of silencing can become political ones when oppressed groups find that, "Whatever is unnamed . . . will become, not merely unspoken, but unspeakable" (199). Ng demonstrates both the subtlety and power of the forces ensuring women's silence and muting their suffering, especially around issues of motherhood. Although Ng's novel is set at the same time *Woman Warrior* was written, her themes have contemporary resonance in our current #MeToo era. Despite popular acclaim, Ng and other authors discussed here have received scant academic attention; this book also attempts, therefore, to break that silence.

The third chapter again compares a classic novel from the 1970s to a contemporary one with a parallel plot line. Toni Morrison's 1977 novel *Song of*

Solomon and Jesmyn Ward's 2017 novel *Sing, Unburied, Sing* both follow Black men on road trips to uncover their familial history. More significantly, both connect their characters' personal epiphanies about racial and gendered expectations to the aftermath of the Great Migration and the legacy of slavery in the American South. Morrison shows Black men responding to ongoing racial oppression with the same methods enslaved people once did: violence, escape, or accumulating wealth. All of these fail to secure liberation, succeeding only in turning Black men against themselves and each other. Rewriting Morrison's tale for the modern era, Ward depicts struggles with poverty, drug addiction, and the prison industrial complex. Embodying a new and less rigid kind of masculinity, her protagonist seems poised to break the familial cycle of incarceration and the even more insidious mentality of enslavement through compassion and care. Both novels emphasize the importance of women as helpers, companions, and teachers to help build a more healing community. Their pilgrimages illuminate not only the distances we have traveled historically but also the progress yet to be made.

The fourth chapter pairs fiction by Latinas from similar working-class backgrounds. Sandra Cisneros's 1984 classic, *The House on Mango Street*, and Kali Fajardo-Anstine's two works, 2019's *Sabrina and Corina* and 2022's *Woman of Light*, follow young Chicanas as they negotiate coming of age in an increasing awareness of disparate class positions. Focusing on the middle-American big cities of their youths, Chicago and Denver respectively, both authors are centrally concerned with changing neighborhoods and the processes of gentrification and ghettoization that disproportionately impact women of color. They both suggest that a successful community response can occur through storytelling and writing—communities that can transcend neighborhoods and class distinctions. Despite accolades for both her short story collection and first novel, including the honor of National Book Award finalist, Kali Fajardo-Anstine has been the subject of little scholarship thus far, making this book one of the first to give an in-depth consideration to her works.

The fifth chapter considers what is at stake if we fail to listen to these literary conversations of historically marginalized people. What do we lose if we continue to think of novels as "solitary births," rather than integrally connected conversations? It models this process by applying each of the previous topics to the authors from a different chapter, considering how narratives of silence impact bilingual characters in Chicana fiction; how stereotypical masculinity looks different for Asian men than for Black men; and how shifting neighborhood dynamics can lead to racial as well as economic segregation. It argues that it is incumbent upon us to read widely and deeply, because fiction can help us cross these borders of identity and motivate us to take action in a way no other medium can. In fact, the myriad fractures that threaten contemporary American society may only be healed by a new form of radical empathy.

Chapter One

The Case for Radical
Empathy in Fiction

Isn't this where empathy begins? Other countries stop seeming quite so "foreign," or inanimate, or strange, when we listen to the intimate voices of their citizens . . . If poetry comes out of the deepest places in the human soul and experience, shouldn't it be as important to learn about one another's poetry, country to country, as one another's weather or gross national products? It seems critical to me. It's another way to study geography!

—Naomi Shihab Nye, "Lights in the Windows"

WHY RADICAL EMPATHY?

If literature can bring us the "intimate voices" of those we consider "foreign," as poet Naomi Shihab Nye suggests above, how else might it impact our world? Yet reading has its enemies. Consider the controversial Common Core standards of 2014, which mandated that 70% of high school reading be non-fiction, and which were defended by their author, David Coleman, with these memorable words: "as you grow up in this world you realize people really don't give a shit about what you feel or what you think" (Tyre). Even those with less extreme views on the matter may dismiss the importance of fiction, as it is tempting in troubled times to focus on the stark reality of seemingly more pressing problems. While fiction will continue to be derided in favor of so-called hard facts or denigrated as escapist child's play, we would do well to consider its value. In a lecture to a girls' school in 1926, Virginia Woolf does so eloquently:

It is true that we get nothing whatsoever except pleasure from reading; it is true that the wisest of us is unable to say what that pleasure may be. But that pleasure—mysterious, unknown, useless as it is—is enough. That pleasure is so curious, so complex, so immensely fertilizing to the mind of anyone who enjoys it, and so wide in its effects, that it would not be in the least surprising to discover, on the day of judgment when secrets are revealed and the obscure is made plain, that the reason why we have grown from pigs to men and women, and come out from our caves, and dropped our bows and arrows, and sat round the fire and talked and drunk and made merry and given to the poor and helped the sick and made pavements and houses and erected some sort of shelter and society on the waste of the world, is nothing but this: we have loved reading. (52)

True to form, Woolf contradicts herself delightfully here, giving us one answer and then another. Reading, she claims, is simultaneously a hedonistic playground *and* essential mental fertilizer; its very role as a pleasure pursuit creates civilization, culture, "society on the waste of the world." It is this last contention that interests me most: the leap from an activity of sheer enjoyment into social consciousness and action. I believe fiction forms this bridge by connecting us with strangers, people truly distanced from our own lives, whose experiences we can experience as our own. Fiction can bring us radical empathy.

I use "radical empathy" to indicate a transformative sense of connection with the other—one that changes how a person views that other enough to change future interactions they may have, and, potentially, help them become more aware of their ability to enact social change for the greater good. Since I first gave Regis University's Faculty Lecture of the Year on this topic in 2019, the term has gained some popularity; it appears in a podcast, various internet articles, and in a book title by Terri E. Givens. A political scientist and founder of The Center for Higher Education Leadership, Givens defines "radical empathy" as "encouraging each of us not only to understand the feelings of others, but also to be motivated to create the change that will allow all of us to benefit from economic prosperity and develop the social relationships that are beneficial to our emotional wellbeing" (1). She emphasizes the necessity of understanding the foundational causes of systemic racism, and that "having empathy is different from practicing empathy" (15). Hillary Clinton also applies radical empathy to political consciousness in her 2018 graduation speech at Yale University: "Healing our country is going to take what I call 'radical empathy,' as hard as it is. This is a moment to reach across divides of race, class, and politics to try to see the world through the eyes of people very different from ourselves and to return to rational debate, to find a way to disagree without being disagreeable, to try to recapture a sense of community" (Gonzalez). Clinton here connects empathy to politics as a means of overcoming the nation's ever-increasing divisiveness. Her definition explicitly offers an understanding of our "common humanity" as a method to overcome conflict (Gonzalez). Other academics have adapted the term to their own disciplines, including anthropologist Ray Turner. Turner explains that those who value cultural sustainability should practice "deep observed, critical, participatory action and research, rooted in radical empathy. From this vantage point practitioners can act and work in ways that sustain culture rather than transposing or dissecting it, and act and work in authentic solidarity with those we are with, in a relationship of care" (33). This method, he argues, can avoid the imperialist or colonialist implications that cultural anthropologists may unwittingly perpetuate. Finally, Judith Jordan, assistant professor of psychiatry at Harvard Medical School and the founding theorist of Relational Cultural Theory, offers a pedagogical example relevant to any teacher. When a student describes being racially profiled, a teacher might "disclose that even though she has read about racial profiling and taught about it for years, that her visceral understanding of the pain caused by racial profiling has deepened by hearing this story from the student. Radical empathy involves radical acceptance of vulnerability, an openness to being affected by one another" (Jordan).[1] The professor in this scenario is more effective if she proves both willing to engage in difficult conversations about otherness and capable of listening genuinely to a different perspective. In all of these contexts, "radical empathy" appears as a way to connect an emotion towards others to action and activism for the common good.

While radical empathy has been applied to these various fields of politics, anthropology, and pedagogy, the practice has not so far become an integral part of teaching or reading fiction. We might draw from these other fields to do so. For example, Turner's approach translates well from anthropology to literature, claiming that through narrative, "ways of participatory knowing . . . become indispensable and foundational as the radical space where we invite one another 'to be' with one another" (33). Narratives, particularly fictional ones, can offer us infinite possibilities of "participatory knowing"; we can broaden our perspectives as far as an author can take us. Though she uses different terminology, Paula Moya provides an excellent example of a move towards this approach to fiction in her 2002 book, *Learning from Experience: Minority Identities, Multicultural Struggles*. Moya defines herself as a "realist," validating personal experience as one component part of understanding an objective reality. Her work demonstrates the potential for literary depictions of such experiences to transcend differences in identity positions. Analyzing Helena Viramontes's novel, *Under the Feet of Jesus*, Moya writes in her introduction:

By encouraging her readers to enter into a relationship of empathic identifi-
cation with Estrella and her family and by exposing them to the moral and
epistemic blindness of those Americans who would view migrant farmworkers
as outsiders to American society, Viramontes implicitly invites her readers to
transcend their own particular perspectives, to complicate their own previous
understandings of the world, and to reach for a less partial, more objective
understanding of our shared world. (20)

This paragraph eloquently describes the importance of empathic identifica-
tion, but later in the book Moya makes a slight change that turns the focus
towards radical empathy. The same paragraph later recurs, but Moya replaces
the final words, "our shared world," with more specific terminology: "the
exploitative economic system in which we all participate" (209). This altera-
tion in wording draws attention to the way the novel models its character's
transformative empathic revelation, and in so doing may inspire readers
towards empathically motivated social action of their own.

Moya goes on to demonstrate the effectiveness of Viramontes's narrative
style by contrasting its focalization with that of William Faulkner, an author
whose efforts to create internally perspectival fiction for intersectional char-
acters were so groundbreaking that their influence on this book and the books
discussed herein is pervasive. Moya observes that Viramontes's novel, *Under
the Feet of Jesus*, shares more with Faulkner's *The Sound and the Fury* than
with that of other Chicanas to whom she is often compared, but with a crucial
difference. *The Sound and the Fury*'s ever-enduring Black servant, Dilsey,
has a section devoted to her, but not internally narrated by her as is the case
for the three Compson sons. This distances the reader from the only principal
female character of color, whereas, Moya observes, Viramontes focalizes her
entire novel through the perspective of Mexican migrant farm workers. Greg
Chase makes a similar argument about how Jesmyn Ward translates William
Faulkner: "Ward may feel, in other words, that her project of representing
the psyches of poor Mississippians owes a debt to Faulkner. But . . . Ward's
own work becomes a means not just of supplementing Faulkner's legacy but
also of correcting its racial blind spots" (201). For both Moya and Chase,
these women writers of color change, expand, elaborate on Faulkner's work;
each step in this literary chain can help lead the reader, in turn, towards both
compassion and action.

Moya views Viramontes's working-class protagonist, Estrella, as exactly
the kind of reader we all should strive to be: one whose empathic identi-
fication leads her to take action against her exploiters. Moya explains this
transformative process for the protagonist: "She merges and incorporates the
others' diverse perspectives into her analysis (or 'reading') of the situation
and experiences a transformation of consciousness that provides her with a

more objective understanding than she previously had of her own and her family's situation of exploitation" (205). Estrella comes to understand that a certain unsympathetic nurse gains privilege by exploiting families like Estrella's own, inspiring her, finally, to fight back. When the nurse refuses to help Estrella's dying companion, she smashes the woman's desk trinkets and photos of her children. Her action is violent, but effective, paralleling many protests that have damaged property to advocate for saving lives. The book's focalization on a young migrant girl grants many readers empathic identification with a different way of life, and its story models for us how empathy can lead to action for the greater good.

Farah Jasmine Griffin's 2021 book, *Read Until You Understand*, takes a more personal approach by connecting works of Black literature to the author's own life story. In keeping with the principles of radical empathy, it emphasizes how literature can lead to activism. Organized around universal themes that all touch on Black oppression (love, beauty, mercy, death), the book uses the literary texts to incite readers to "rethink their notion of what the United States is and their place within it and within the world" (XI). At every turn, Griffin notes both the impact these works have had on her personally, and their potential to create social change, saying, "the stories that I tell, the literature that I share, and the values it explores remain urgent and necessary" (XII). Throughout the book she uses the term "ethic of care," which bears some similarity to my use of "radical empathy." Griffin explains how the MacTeer children in Toni Morrison's first novel, *The Bluest Eye*, grow into and through their generosity and kindness towards their outcast friend, Pecola: "They are nurtured in love and governed by an ethic of care. And they are transformed in the act of caring for one in need of it" (12). In contrast, she notes how the book indicts those (nearly all of "respectable" adult society) who reject and abandon Pecola, leading to her descent into madness. Even the well-meaning Black community thus unconsciously reinforces White patriarchal hegemony. And so, she concludes, "The novel, in telling that story, becomes a tool, a weapon, in that ongoing war" (12). She demonstrates her own "ethic of care" when she goes on to imagine Phillis Wheatley's life as an enslaved girl, attempting to give one of our earliest known Black poets a depth and personhood beyond what we can learn from the historical record. How can we imagine her humanity and continue to allow slavery—forced labor, exploitation, and human trafficking—in our contemporary world? The works of Black literature have a visceral, enduring impact on Griffin; she proposes that they may also inspire resistance to White supremacy and other global injustices.

As much as literature has the capacity to open our understanding of others, we should remain mindful of the inherent limitations of empathic awareness. Saidiya Hartman warns of the dangers of believing we can fully understand the pain of the oppressed: "empathy fails to expand the space of the other but merely places the self in its stead" (20). Total identification with someone else's experience is both implausible, due to our unique psyches and myriad shifting identity positions, and undesirable, as it would erode important distinctions and differences. Jean Wyatt provides a useful model of how literature can help us engage empathically with social justice while also continuing to demarcate difference when necessary. In *Risking Difference: Identification, Race, and Community in Contemporary Fiction and Feminism*, Wyatt points out the benefit of combining seemingly disparate theoretical approaches because, as she asks rhetorically, "how can desire and identification be separated from power relations, or the individual psyche from cultural formations?" (5). She argues, as I do, for the importance of literature to help us "identify with the cultural other to some degree" (9). She reminds us that no such identification can be total; we must be able to relate to the other without believing we can *become* the other, thus valuing the "other's perspective without usurping or destroying it" (171). This is a distinction Trinh T. Minh-ha further complicates in her essay "Not You/Like You" by deconstructing the boundaries between self and other, insider and outsider. Minh-ha explains that "the moment the insider steps out from the inside she's no longer a mere insider," instead, she is simultaneously "affirming 'I am like you' while persisting in her difference and that of reminding 'I am different' while unsettling every definition of otherness arrived at" (Minh-ha). Like Wyatt and Minh-ha, I am advocating in this book for understanding that leads to change, not for the impossible task of completely merging the viewpoints of self and other.

Wyatt demonstrates her critical process through an analysis of Cherríe Moraga's autobiographical essay, "From a Long Line of *Vendidas*"—which Wyatt notably defines as a "dialogue," emphasizing the crucial exchange between reader and writer that I advocate here. Wyatt connects deeply to Moraga's pain at feeling less loved than her brother, which Wyatt experienced herself but also recognizes as differing due to their respective cultures. Moraga describes how her Chicana background shapes her view of gender roles by consistently implying that "you are a traitor to your race if you do not put the man first" (qtd. in Wyatt 174). Wyatt has a point of entry to Moraga's worldview because she has experienced similar family dynamics; she also recognizes that her own cultural background makes this experience different. A fluid dynamic thus emerges between author and reader: "identification is not uniform and all consuming, but shifting: I am like her, then not her, moving in and out, making a partial identification" (174). Moya reads Viramontes as revising Faulkner to give voice to an underrepresented individual; Wyatt reads Moraga and rewrites her own experience as both similar and different.

In each case, books build off one another and inspire authors to hear another's story and revise, rethink, recreate their own.

FROM FICTION TO ACTION

This process of using literature to create more literature, of remaking a text in the reading of it, is famously defined by Julia Kristeva's 1966 essay "Word, Dialogue and Novel" as "intertextuality." Kristeva, following Bakhtin, advocates viewing "the 'literary word' as an *intersection of textual surfaces* rather than a *point* (a fixed meaning), as a dialogue among several writings" (65). She discusses the many possible intersections between reader/writer and text/context, observing that they create "a mosaic of quotations; any text is the absorption and transformation of another" (66). "Intertextuality" has expanded from Kristeva's original semiotic use involving the "transposition of systems or signs" (15) and is now frequently used in a broader sense, as I do here, to connote texts that impact, reference, and speak to one another. Kristeva also explicitly links this rhetorical practice to activism. In the same essay, she advocates for Bakhtin's view of the potential of literature to be transgressive, noting that his "carnivalesque discourse breaks through the laws of a language censored by grammar and semantics and, at the same time, is a social and political protest" (65). Looking at the way texts impact other texts—some intended by the author, some not—can demonstrate literature's power to disrupt and change.

One illuminating example of intertextuality as a path to radical empathy is Azar Nafisi's book about teaching books, *Reading Lolita in Tehran.* Nafisi's writing absorbs classical works of British and American literature and transforms them into literature of resistance to the oppressive regime of the Ayatollah Khomeni, under which small children are "punished for wearing colored shoelaces, for running in the schoolyard, for licking ice cream in public" (67). She teaches American novels, not for their escapism into a presumably freer society, but because by shedding light on the universality of totalitarianism, they help promote activism: "Curiously, the novels we escaped into led us finally to question and prod our own realities, about which we felt so helplessly speechless" (38–39). It is this step, from fiction to action, that gives Nafisi and her students both the will and the courage to defy their regime; the books, and the Iranian girls' collective interpretation of them, radicalizes their empathy.

Though Nafisi discusses many texts, *Lolita* is the central and eponymous one because it so eloquently depicts the plight of someone vulnerable at the hands of someone powerful. This is a situation familiar to all Nafisi's students, who are beaten and jailed for crimes straight out of Margaret Atwood's

The Handmaid's Tale, such as being suspected of wearing makeup or appearing in public with a male. Reading *Lolita* in Iran is not, Nafisi suggests, an act of wishful thinking, of imagining themselves into a liberated America; rather, it links young women in Iran to victimized Lolita herself. Nafisi's book, in turn, links students worldwide of all backgrounds back to the country she left behind. Nafisi observes that Lolita, at thirteen, would not be an abducted child in Iran, but a perfectly legal child-bride since the age of nine. How can students in that world identify with Lolita's abuse, when she indulges in the liberties of saddle shoes and swimsuits, ice cream parlors and summer camps, and they may be expected to spend their childhoods bearing children? They can understand because oppression, Nafisi contends, translates through the medium of fiction, even as it transforms for each reader in our own particular circumstances.

Scientists agree, as empirical studies have confirmed both that fiction helps create empathy and that people with higher empathy are often readers. In November 2014, a Carnegie Mellon team studied the fMRI brain activity of subjects while they read a section of *Harry Potter* describing his experience of flying for the first time. First author Leila Wehbe summarizes her findings: "It turns out that movement of the characters—such as when they are flying their brooms—is associated with activation in the same brain region that we use to perceive other people's motion. Similarly, the characters in the story are associated with activation in the same brain region we use to process other people's intentions" (qtd. in Spice). Her study concludes that our brains experience fiction not just empathically, but *as though it is happening.* We feel Harry's flight, or Lolita's pain, as though it were our own. A study published around the same time, "Can Classic Moral Stories Promote Honesty in Children?" answered its titular question: yes. The University of Toronto researchers and their collaborators "found that reading a child a fictional story about honesty led the child to act more honestly when presented with a situation in which he or she could lie or cheat" (Lee et al). They found that "George Washington and the Cherry Tree" was more effective for this purpose than "Pinocchio" or "The Boy Who Cried Wolf," likely because it emphasized honesty as positive rather than dishonesty as negative. Suzanne Keen took this research one step further and proved that fiction can lead from an empathic response to altruistic behavior through what she calls "the literary version of the empathy-altruism hypothesis, which holds that novel reading, by eliciting empathy, encourages prosocial action and good world citizenship" (224). All of these studies demonstrate the power for literature to create social change.

History, of course, provides a long record of novels that have led to social change. We might think of how Harriet Beecher Stowe's *Uncle Tom's Cabin* spurred the cause of abolitionism, famously leading President Lincoln to remark upon meeting her, "So you're the little woman who wrote the book that started this great war" (Harriet Beecher Stowe Center). We may remember that Upton Sinclair's *The Jungle* transformed the meat-packing industry and helped create the Food and Drug Adminstration, or that George Orwell's *1984* incited opposition to totalitarianism and gave us a whole new vocabulary to do so. In each case, I believe the crucial process involved was that those books allowed readers to empathize with people unlike themselves, as Nafisi's students learned to do with Lolita. Becoming invested in the greater good requires the capacity to imagine that it is our own loved one felled by gunfire at a school; our own parent dying, untreated, at home; our own child stolen from our arms and incarcerated on the border; our own planet dying by degrees from wanton carelessness. If we cannot conceive of the problems of others as though they were our own, even and especially when they could never be our own, they remain unconquerable. Fiction, in contrast, allows us an opportunity: rather than seeing the lives of others as fleeting wisps from news headlines pock-mocked with disasters, we can vicariously live the lives of those most unlike us.

STORIES OF STRANGERS

Fiction allows us the unique experience of connecting with more strangers than we could ever meet in one lifetime. Of course, all our intimates were strangers once. Tolstoy's Anna Karenina and Count Vronsky meet as strangers on a train, and their lives transform through their destructive passion. Runaway Huck Finn encounters runaway enslaved man Jim, and fugitives become friends. But there are also strangers who never become intimate— those who leave but a scratch on a life, and yet, that scratch transforms. Ralph Ellison's 1952 *Invisible Man* is a book of encounters with such strangers, recounting how the unnamed and impressionable protagonist evolves through meeting veterans and preachers, union men and their opposition, gamblers, Communists, and yam venders. One of the first and most significant of these incidences occurs when, as a Black college student in the segregated South, he chauffeurs the wealthy, White Mr. Norton. The Invisible Man makes worlds collide by introducing Mr. Norton to an impoverished Black sharecropper, Trueblood, and soon his own path swerves from its marching band step into a loose jazz riff that he improvises for the rest of the novel. The Invisible Man's tune changes slightly with each encounter; he goes from blandly mouthing the pablum of Black people's "social responsibility" to White authority to inciting crowds to riot against evictions and inequality (30). For Ellison, ephemeral encounters with strangers are not peripheral, but essential: perhaps all the more so when they are fleeting. While such examples abound, I will discuss two from works that not only depict centrally significant encounters with strangers but also speak metatextually to the importance of passing those stories on through narrative and art.

A chance encounter lies at the heart of William Faulkner's 1936 masterpiece, *Absalom, Absalom!*, which envisions its characters becoming not only interested in, but virtually one with, the story they hear and tell.[2] This story of storytelling describes how each of its narrators becomes obsessed with a complex legend of a Civil War icon, which becomes a tale of the American South, which becomes a narrative of racism and sacrifice and God and endurance and obsession. At the heart of this story-within-stories lies a crucial encounter between strangers in which Judith Sutpen gifts a personal letter to a distant neighbor. Judith explains that we are all trying to weave our own pattern on the loom of fate, though the threads entangle with others, ensnaring us: "Read it if you like or don't read it if you like. Because you make so little impression, you see. You get born and you try this and you don't know why only you keep on trying it and you are born at the same time with a lot of other people, all mixed up with them, like trying to, having to, move your arms and legs with string only the same strings are hitched to all the other arms and legs" (100–101). The passage suggests that although our strings entangle, there is still a loom—still weaving—still art. Our individual craftsmanship appears incomprehensible until viewed as within and part of the larger pattern. The very process of sharing her letter, Judith goes on to explain, weaves her pattern into the larger loom: "If you could go to someone, the stranger the better, and give them something—a scrap of paper—something, anything, it not to mean anything in itself and them not even to read it or keep it, not even bother to throw it away or destroy it, at least it would be something just because it would have happened, be remembered" (100). According to Judith, such a connection must be made to those *outside* our closest circles—"the stranger the better." Closed circles prove pernicious in Faulkner's world; incest recurs as a metaphor for the post–Civil War South that could never break the cyclical immolations of its own self-obsessed history. Here, he goes further to imply the need for radical empathy—the need for every Judith to pass along a puzzling letter for no other purpose, and with no other expectation, than the crucial act of connection to another human.

Years later, that letter passes on to the woman's grandson, Quentin Compson. The tale engulfs him, consumes him, until he brings it North to his chilly dorm-room at Harvard, and its telling weaves him homoerotically close with his best and perhaps only friend, Shreve. Shreve will outlive Quentin and bear the story further North, to his native Canada, and of course Faulkner's novel will take it further still, translated into languages worldwide, reprinted decades later. The story of Judith's letter thus becomes emblematic of the process I analyze throughout this book: one text leads readers to think outside themselves; those readers write their own stories, literally or figuratively; more people are expanded by this understanding of someone different from themselves; and a more empathic and engaged population results.

Faulkner's work found its way through time to another stranger: Toni Morrison. Morrison wrote her master's thesis on Faulkner, and she shares Faulkner's interest in giving voice to myriad internalized perspectives. *Beloved*, like *Absalom, Absalom!*, is a Civil War narrative that demonstrates the importance of storytelling as testimony to historical traumas and their aftershocks. Sethe often tells her daughter Denver her agonizing birth story; Denver retells it to her reincarnated dead sister, Beloved; and finally Sethe's memory is told only to the reader. The story vividly gains life through this process: "And the more fine points [Denver] made, the more detail she provided, the more Beloved liked it. So she anticipated the questions by giving blood to the scraps her mother and grandmother had told her—and a heartbeat. The monologue became, in fact, a duet" (92). Beloved herself, a ghost murdered by her mother to avoid re-enslavement, is scraps given blood through storytelling. Beloved haunts the house until Sethe's memory of her becomes so powerful as to render Beloved corporeal again, and soon she begins devouring the lives of her mother and sister in an insatiable hunger. Yet she both sustains and is sustained by Denver's birth story. In the "duet" they create, the story we read becomes a fiction of a fiction: Morrison's imagined recounting of an enslaved girl embellishing the story her mother told her. But in its brutality, the story conveys what must have been the lived truth for many enslaved people. It connects present-day readers to a past they could not otherwise imagine.

The birth story describes how Sethe, whipped nearly to death, encountered a stranger: a runaway indentured servant, scarecrow-thin and wild-haired, dreaming of velvet and Boston and spewing stories with unfiltered loquacity. Despite being brutally taught to trust no one, Sethe later recollects that this White girl, Amy Denver, gained her confidence because of her "fugitive eyes and her tenderhearted mouth" (92). Amy takes Sethe's battered Black feet in her White hands and massages them back to health, an act of devotion, as she assures Sethe that the pain can resurrect: "Anything dead coming back to life hurts" (42). She heals the scars from Sethe's abusive slave master with cobwebs, a natural magic that converts the spider's death-trap into a soothing balm. Yet her true balm is literary, as she rewrites Sethe's gruesome scar into vital, arboreal, beauty: "See, here's the trunk—it's red and split wide open, full of sap, and this here's the parting for the branches. You got a mighty lot of branches. Leaves, too, look like, and dern if these ain't blossoms. Tiny little cherry blossoms, just as white. Your back got a whole tree on it. In bloom" (93). Amy gives a stranger the gift of this fiction, transforming her bloodied scars into something lovely, life-giving, even fruitful. Fleeing alone, Sethe could—to steal a line from T.S. Eliot, "neither stand nor lie nor sit," immobilized by her scar-riddled back and baby-laden front ("The Waste Land")—yet Amy's fiction begins the process of delivering her from both pains. Together the two strangers have created life:

> On a riverbank in the cool of a summer evening two women struggled under a shower of silvery blue. They never expected to see each other again in this world and at the moment couldn't care less. But there on a summer night surrounded by bluefern they did something together appropriately and well. A pateroller passing would have sniggered to see two throw-away people, two lawless outlaws—a slave and a barefoot whitewoman with unpinned hair—wrapping a ten-minute-old baby in the rags they wore. (99–100)

Sethe finds but fleeting respite, like the brief cool in the Southern summer evening, in the arms of a stranger; further devastations await her on the free side of the Ohio River. But Morrison invokes the shadow of the pateroller— a slave patroller—as an externalized perspective to what the reader knows. Amy and Sethe, strong and kind, are no "throw-away people"; they are outside the law only because the law declares them outsiders. Morrison gestures towards a different kind of law in her phrase "appropriately and well," repeated twice for effect, suggesting that these adolescent girls obey a superseding moral code. In an agony-soaked novel, this moment brings solace and relief. Each woman connected with a stranger, despite the considerable risk, and grows from the connection.

AVOIDING THE SINGLE STORY

So too can we, as readers, grow from our connections to strangers through literature. To do so requires a wide variety of narratives, however, as no single author can speak for an entire category of people. Toni Morrison is the only African American to have won a Nobel prize; as Namwalli Serpell observes, "she is our only truly canonical black, female writer" (Serpell). This book's approach of pairing a "canonical" female author of color with a later one, sharing her background and influenced by her work but taking it in new directions, attempts to move beyond the inherent limitations of any singular perspective. By doing so we understand the chain of influence from one novel to another, and simultaneously ensure that no author's singular narrative becomes monolithic. Nigerian author Chimimanda Adichie advises how we can avoid this "danger of the single story" through reading many. She concludes her TEDtalk on the subject with this summary:

Stories matter. Many stories matter. Stories have been used to dispossess and to malign, but stories can also be used to empower and to humanize. Stories can break the dignity of a people, but stories can also repair that broken dignity. The American writer Alice Walker wrote this about her Southern relatives who had moved to the North. She introduced them to a book about the Southern life that they had left behind. "They sat around, reading the book themselves, listening to me read the book, and a kind of paradise was regained." I would like to end with this thought: That when we reject the single story, when we realize that there is never a single story about any place, we regain a kind of paradise. (17:24–18:18)

One narrative is only a beginning—regaining paradise requires us to understand other cultures when we have access to multiple narratives from multiple perspectives. Adichie is, of course, not the only author to combat the danger of the single story. Maxine Hong Kingston, one of the first canonized Asian American woman writers, stated in a 1980 interview, "What I look forward to is the time when many of us are published and then we will be able to see the range of personalities and the range of viewpoints, of visions, of what it is to be a Chinese American" (*Conversations* 21). Thirty years later, we might hope that this situation has changed, but contemporary novelist Celeste Ng argues otherwise. She writes that even today critics assume that authors like herself can write only "A Story About Being Chinese, not stories about families, love, loss, or universal human experience" (*Huffington Post*). The "human experience" cannot be "universal" if it is exclusionary; yet so often writers outside the margins are expected to stay there. As Maxine Hong Kingston's fictional playwright describes his reviewers, "They think they know us—the wide range of us from sweet to sour—because they eat in Chinese restaurants . . . they've got us in a bag we aren't punching our way out of" (*Tripmaster* 308). In other words, Asian American writers may be welcomed only so long as they spice their sentences with miso or masala and clothe their conclusions in kimonos or saris. This book engages writers of similar cultural backgrounds, writing about the same topic, to explore the complex differences in the stories they have to tell.

Countering the Single Story narrative involves not only complicating "A Story About Being Chinese," for example, but also considering when a Chinese story might better be compared to a Mexican or African one. For example, Jhumpa Lahiri and Salman Rushdie may be two of the most famous writers of Indian heritage, but just as Moya links Viramontes to Faulkner rather than Cisneros, I would argue that Lahiri's Kolkata owes more to Henry James, while Salman Rushdie's Mumbai is closer kin to James Joyce. In her book on Black literature, Farah Jasmine Griffin writes similarly: "I continued to read Black authors, who I now placed in conversation with the revered white ones I encountered in school. Wasn't James Baldwin's *Go Tell It on the*

Mountain similar to *A Portrait of the Artist?*" (19). I would agree that it is, but this kind of comparison appears counterintuitive to many. As Celeste Ng wryly observes in *The Huffington Post*: "somewhere in the Commandments of Reviewing must be written: *Thou shalt not compare Asians to non-Asians.*" This book, and hopefully others like it, breaks that commandment by seeking connection both within and beyond cultural backgrounds to avoid the danger of the Single Story for any given ethnicity. For this reason, this book's final chapter considers cross-cultural connections that demonstrate how the themes discussed in the earlier chapters are applicable to authors across multiple color lines.

INTERSECTIONALITY: THERE IS NO SINGLE STORY

In addition to discussing complexities within an identity group and connec-tions between different ones, this book seeks to analyze all identity positions as intersectional. Kimberlé Crenshaw coined the term "intersectionality" in her 1989 legal analysis of violence against Black women: "Although racism and sexism readily intersect in the lives of real people, they seldom do in feminist and antiracist practices. And so, when the practices expound identity as woman or person of color as an either/or proposition, they relegate the identity of women of color to a location that resists telling" (1242). This essay has helped scholars across disciplines consider identity as complex and inter-connected, avoiding the "either/or" thinking Crenshaw describes. Patricia Hill Collins built on this work, elaborating in *Black Feminist Thought* on how oppression can form a structural "matrix" that includes class and sexuality as well as race and gender: "The matrix of dominations refers to how these intersecting oppressions are actually organized. Regardless of the particular intersections involved, structural, disciplinary, hegemonic, and interpersonal domains of power reappear across quite different forms of oppression" (18). Re-envisioning oppression through the lens of the matrix, rather than as a series of individual points, gives a more realistic and holistic sense of dis-crimination. Originally used to consider Black women specifically, the term "intersectionality" began to expand to include multiple identity positions. This word now has a wide (arguably, too wide) usage far beyond its initial context, so I will specify the way I'm applying it here.

I use intersectionality to describe the way that everyone's identities con-nect and overlap, so that, for example, Audre Lorde's experience as a Black queer woman is not simply the sum of those parts but a unique blend of them impacted and influenced by larger systems of oppression. This reading accords with the 2015 definition of intersectionality in the Oxford English

Dictionary and, perhaps more importantly, with that of the accurately self-proclaimed "bible of women of color feminism," *This Bridge Called My Back* ("Catching Fire" xxii). In the preface to the 2015 edition, Cherríe Moraga defines intersectionality as the place "where multiple identities converge at the crossroads of a woman of color life," ("Catching Fire" xxii) and later applies it to her own experience: "The joys of looking like a white girl ain't so great since I realized I could be beaten on the street for being a dyke" ("La Güera" 24). Ange-Marie Hancock's *Intersectionality: An Intellectual History* offers a similar perspective, emphasizing that the goal of intersectional scholarship is both to deepen our knowledge of "between-category relationships" (33) and also to bring increased visibility to those who have too often been underrepresented—both of which are central objectives of this book. Christie Launius and Holly Hassel, both Women's Studies professors at the University of Wisconsin, likewise focus on the interplay between private experience and societal hierarchies, explaining that categories such as gender, race, and class "intersect at the micro level of individual experience to reflect multiple interlocking systems of privilege and oppression at the macro, social-structural level" (114–15). Every author speaks from a particular intersectional position complexly composed of race, gender, class, sexuality, and so forth; similarly, a novel can consider the intersectional identities of its separate characters while also weaving together racism, sexism, classism, and homophobia to illuminate structures of privilege and their impact. Novels in fact give us a particular view into multiple simultaneous societal dynamics we might not be able to access in any other way.

To demonstrate this process at work, we might consider the 2017 novel *The Ministry of Utmost Happiness* by Indian writer-turned-activist Arundhati Roy. The book features a high-born transgender woman of color whose identity is made up of and more than each of these descriptions. Born intersex, the protagonist chooses the female name Anjum, meaning "stars," rejecting her male dead name, Aftab, meaning "sun"—the homonym of which connotes a male child as well. Her process of transitioning from Aftab to Anjum, from sun to stars, begins with an encounter with a stranger like those previously discussed. Upon seeing "a tall, slim-hipped woman wearing bright lipstick, gold high heels and a shiny, green satin salwar kameez buying bangles," Aftab feels an immediate connection and new identity awareness: "he wanted to be her" (23), implying the woman he sees, but also a "her" more generally speaking. Longing to follow this woman's path, Aftab begins by literally following her path. Upon losing sight of her, he reflects, "No ordinary woman would have been permitted to sashay down the streets of Shahjahanabad dressed like that. Ordinary women in Shahjahanabad wore burqas or at least covered their heads and every part of their body except their hands and feet. The woman Aftab followed could dress as she was dressed and walk the way she did only because she wasn't a woman" (22). The woman who is "no ordinary woman" is Bombay Silk, a *Hijra*, a term Indians use to denote those who are not born with two X chromosomes but choose to present as female. Honored in Hindu mythology for their loyalty to Lord Rama during his time in exile, they are the oldest known transgender community and are believed to have the power of both blessings and curses. They were well accepted in society until the British colonizers infiltrated the country and its morals with their own version of sexual propriety. However, in 2014, India's Supreme Court recognized transgender people as a Third Gender, granting them full legal rights (Gettleman). All of this, however, is conveyed to readers in a very different way through Roy's characters than through a mere listing of historical facts.

Anjum eventually joins Bombay Silk's brothel, *Kwabgah*, meaning "House of Dreams," and so it becomes: Anjum finds happiness, belonging, and a narrative in which changing genders is merely a chapter, not the sum total of her experience. Fiction has the power to enable us to see marginality as significant, perhaps defining, but not exclusively so. Roy accomplishes this by depicting many *hijra* characters with myriad experiences. For example, Anjum's friend Nimmo mocks her complacent contentment:

> No one's happy here. It's not possible. Arre yaar, think about it, what are the things you normal people get unhappy about? Price-rise, children's school admissions, husbands' beatings, wives' cheatings, Hindu-Muslim riots, Indo-Pak war—outside things that settle down eventually. But for us the price-rise and school-admissions and beating-husbands and cheating-wives are all inside us. The riot is inside us. The war is inside us. Indo-Pak is inside us. It will never settle down. It can't. (27)

Within one text, Roy defies the single story, making it multiple. Anjum's "house of dreams" is more of a nightmare for Nimmo, and so we see that *hijras* are not all seeking the same concept of home. The characters' intersectional identities reflect the larger power structures of the nation as a whole, as Nimmo shows by linking their internalized division to the fragmentation of the nation: Hindu vs. Muslim, India vs. Pakistan. Anjum claims at one point that she is "all of them" (8); like Walt Whitman, she is "wide, (she) contains multitudes," and the novel must be wide enough to contain her as well. Its author herself contains such multitudes, writing a critically acclaimed novel, then dedicating twenty years of her life to human rights activism, and then returning to write another. Arundhati Roy gives voice to the voiceless, on paper and in protest, and is a model for how we all might do so as well.

CONCLUSION: INTO THE FUTURE

The "Single Story" narrative impacts not only current readers but also future authors. *Hijras* have not made frequent appearances in contemporary fiction, but three years after Roy's book, Megha Majumdar published an excellent debut novel, *A Burning*, told in part from a *hijra*'s viewpoint. The long arms of fiction stretch ever outward, touching strangers who will touch others in turn. In 1929, Virginia Woolf opined in *A Room of One's Own* that valuing women's writing of the present requires studying and appreciating women's writing of the past: "masterpieces are not single and solitary births; they are the outcome of many years of thinking in common, of thinking by the body of the people, so that the experience of the mass is behind the single voice" (65). Tillie Olsen reinforced Virginia Woolf's emphasis on the importance of women's presence within the historical canon at what must have been a pre-dominantly male audience at the Modern Language Association convention in 1971: "Predecessors, ancestors, a body of literature, an acceptance of the right to write: each in themselves an advantage" (23). Near the beginning of our own century Naomi Lowinsky acknowledged the conflict many women feel between their heritage and their own generations but advised that we must not lose sight of the narratives of the past: "stories from the Motherline are as familiar to us as our own lives . . . for a modern woman to root herself in her female lineage, she must honor both the archetypal and historical aspects of her Motherline." (99). She cites Woolf multiple times within her book as well. In 2020 Griffin writes of the way previous Black writers inspired her own writing: "I also had a home in pages and pages of books filled with another kind of legacy—one that stretched far back and seemed to project me into a distant future" (14). Thus, Virginia Woolf, long-ago silenced by death, wrote of the importance of narratives linked across history; this message reached Olsen, and Lowinsky, and Griffin, strangers nearly a century into a future she would never behold.

It is not merely important but exigent that writers like Woolf continue to reach such readers. If we cannot encounter the stranger in fiction, we risk losing our capacity for radical empathy and, thus, our potential to build a more caring and engaged society. As theories of intersectionality suggest, this requires not only attention to novels by and about people of varying race, gender, sexualities, and class positions but also an understanding of the way those identities mutually impact one another and reflect society as we know it.

I will conclude this chapter with a vision of the past foretelling the future. Our aforementioned storyteller of storytelling, William Faulkner, connects the two at the end of his 1950 Nobel Prize acceptance speech.

I believe that man will not merely endure: he will prevail. He is immortal, not because he alone among creatures has an inexhaustible voice, but because he has a soul, a spirit capable of compassion and sacrifice and endurance. The poet's, the writer's, duty is to write about these things. It is his privilege to help man endure by lifting his heart, by reminding him of the courage and honor and hope and pride and compassion and pity and sacrifice which have been the glory of his past. The poet's voice need not merely be the record of man, it can be one of the props, the pillars to help him endure and prevail. (724)

Here, in the devastating wake of a second world war, William Faulkner, miserable alcoholic, philanderer, unhappy in love and in living, unexpectedly turns optimist. Is it a façade, a convenient costume for the laureate's literati? Or a fleeting euphoria born of toiling for decades in obscurity or ridicule before ultimately receiving the highest honor of the literary world? I would argue that Faulkner's works always contained the desperate, frail, tenacious seedlings of hope. It is there in the finale of *Light in August,* when Lena Grove, penniless and pregnant, looks ahead as she travels the South, placid and expectant: "My, my. A body does get around" (507). It is there in *The Sound and the Fury*, whose appendix concludes with Dilsey, the stalwart Black servant, giving the decaying Compson family their only fragile cohesion: "they endured"—not one person, singular, but "they," plural (215). It is there in *Absalom, Absalom!*, in the suggestion that Quentin Compson's epic Civil War story will live past him, past Shreve, into and through all of us.

I believe these seedlings of hope inspired Toni Morrison, and Arundhati Roy, whose works are likewise brutal but hopeful. I hope their radical empathy will inspire you as well. Readers are always strangers to an initial text: We enter a fictional world all unknown. Fiction at its best makes strangers intimates, bringing us asymptotically closer to imagining lives otherwise unimaginable.

NOTES

1. Terri E. Givens also cites "A willingness to be vulnerable" as one of the tenets of radical empathy (21).
2. Faulkner describes two of the narrators, Quentin and Shreve, merging with the story they create as they tell it together: "Now neither of them was there. They were both in Carolina and the time was forty-six years ago . . . Now both of them were Henry Sutpen and both of them were Bon, compounded each of both yet neither either" (280).

Chapter Two

"Not Merely Unspoken, but Unspeakable"

The Silences of Celeste Ng and Maxine Hong Kingston

Death, on the other hand, is the final silence. And that might be coming quickly, now, without regard for whether I had ever spoken what needed to be said, or had only betrayed myself into small silences, while I planned someday to speak, or waited for someone else's words.

—Audre Lorde, "The Transformation of
Silence into Language and Action"

INTRODUCTION: KEEPING QUIET

When author Celeste Ng attended Harvard, what was her personality rating? This odd question was at the heart of the plaintiff's argument in the *Students for Fair Admissions v. Harvard* lawsuit. Harvard's fluid "personal rating" consistently ranks Asian students the lowest, which, according to Diane Wu of *This American Life*, is due to an institutionalized preference for loud applicants over quiet ones: "The words Harvard uses to describe what they're looking for are things like leadership, courage, sense of humor, effervescence. It's like they want to fill the school with future senators, perky Gryffindors, and Reese Witherspoon in *Legally Blonde* types" (Wu). Despite this glib phrasing, Wu and others have called attention to the sinister reality behind the idea of favoring the voluble as a means of coding racism, and thus barring Asians without having to admit it.

Asian-American literary studies have long called attention to this discrimi-
nation based on an alleged lack of ebullience. In *This Bridge Called My Back:
Writings of Radical Women of Color*, Mitsuye Yamada decries the silencing
of Asian American women: "We must remember that one of the most insidi-
ous ways of keeping women and minorities powerless is to let them only talk
about harmless and inconsequential subjects, or let them speak freely and not
listen to them with serious intent. We need to raise our voices a little more"
(35). Yamada notably points to a lack of genuine listening as part of the
silencing process, which removes the onus from the "powerless" and places
it instead on the powerful. In her groundbreaking book devoted to this topic,
Articulate Silences, King-Kok Cheung elaborates on the implicit disempow-
erment of silence:

> Attitudes toward Asian and Asian American reserve have been mostly critical
> or patronizing. The quiet Asians are seen either as devious, timid, shrewd, and,
> above all, "inscrutable"—in much the same way that women are thought to be
> mysterious and unknowable—or as docile, submissive, and obedient, worthy
> of the label "model minority," just as silent women have traditionally been
> extolled. (2)

Silence can thus be perceived as either threatening or ineffectual, but typi-
cally as a marker of powerlessness. In contrast, Cheung goes on to observe
that Asian cultures often value "verbal restraint" and "reticence" (6), and that
"traditional Chinese and Japanese literature . . . generally value the implicit
over the explicit" (8). Many authors have expanded this discussion of the mul-
tiple valences of silence to include women more broadly. According to Elaine
Hedges and Shelley Fisher Fishkin, silences "might reveal reticences cultur-
ally imposed on women . . . or, alternatively, women's deployment of silence
as a form of resistance to dominant discourse" (5). In "The Uses of Silence,"
Patti L. Duncan discusses these multiple valences at length, observing that
"there are qualitative differences between being silent and being *silenced*"
(29), and that "silence functions as a way of saying (and of unsaying) and is
related to ways of seeing (unseeing) and knowing (unknowing)" (30). These
critics collectively reveal that women in general, and Asian American women
in particular, receive conflicting messages about silence. As a result, Cheung
observes that they are often "mediating between a dominant culture that
advertises 'free' speech (but maintains minority silence) and an ethnic one
that insists on the propriety of reticence" (16). Silence can appear simultane-
ously mandated and forbidden by the same patriarchal structures.

In Celeste Ng's acclaimed 2014 novel, *Everything I Never Told You*, every
major character is marginalized, silent, or silenced. While the plot centers
around the drowning of Lydia Lee, the novel's more significant underpinning

is the psychological and sociological factors rooted in the past, and extending into the future. According to Ng, the structure of her novel altered as she was "trying to figure out how to weave past and present together," an effect she only achieved when she began to use the "old-fashioned" omniscient narrator ("Politics and Prose," 40:13, 27:33). She emphasizes the gap between past and present by setting the novel in the 1970s, feeling "there was a real turning point" in opportunities for the marginalized at that time (Ng, "Kirkus" 2:27). Communication styles have changed as well, and she observes that now "we put a value on open communication, on emotional self-analysis, and on voicing fears and insecurities. That wasn't as common a view in the 1960s and 1970s" (Cruz). In this chapter, I examine the racial and gendered silences of Ng's novel by putting it in conversation with writers from the 1970s of its setting, focusing on Maxine Hong Kingston but also addressing Adrienne Rich, Frank Chin, and Audre Lorde, who all discuss similar silencings. I show how Ng achieves a critical distancing from the 1970s through her future-omniscient narrator, highlighting both contemporary progress and extant struggles. By leveraging the past, Ng creates a dramatic irony that grants her readership a particular kind of double vision, one that consciously links the sins of our fathers—and mothers—to the far from perfect world we inherited from them. In so doing, her novel reminds us that unless we can experience radical empathy with those different from us, little will change, and we will continue to privilege the "ebullient" over the quiet without even noticing the racial implications of doing so.

THE SILENCING OF *THE WOMAN WARRIOR*

Ng's 2014 novel, *Everything I Never Told You*, shares a literary lineage with Kingston's seminal 1976 work, *The Woman Warrior.* Both books narrate the story of a Chinese woman who drowns, forcibly silenced by patriarchal forces. The influence of Kingston's memoir to Ng's generation can hardly be overstated; it was, according to David Leiwei Li, "the most widely taught book by a living writer in US colleges and universities" during Ng's Harvard years in the 1990s (qtd in Hall, 176). Acknowledging Kingston's influence, Ng states that she is "grateful to many of the greats like Maxine Hong Kingston" (Gee) and calls *Woman Warrior* "A classic, for a reason" (@ prononced_ing). Despite her avowed respect for Kingston, Ng has publicly objected to being compared to her on the basis of their shared Chinese heritage alone. In 2010, she opined, "Comparing Asian writers mainly to other Asian writers implies that we're all telling the same story—a disappointingly reductive view. It places Asian writers in their own segregated Asians-only pool: you may be funny, but we can't compare you to, say, David Sedaris or

Lorrie Moore—let's see, who's funny and Asian?" (*Huffington Post*). Ng, following Chimamanda Adichie's TED Talk, "The Danger of a Single Story,"[1] believes that the remedy is to expand the single ethnic narrative into multiple stories, so that Kingston no longer bears the burden of being the lone prominent voice of Chinese American women. Ng has worked towards this goal by actively promoting new writers, particularly those of Asian heritage, adding more stories to our collective narrative (Lamy).

While we should resist facile comparison between authors who happen to share a region of origin, there is good reason to consider narrative heritage in literary legacies, especially for women and writers of color. Adrienne Rich made this point about feminist authors in her 1979 forward to *On Lies, Secrets, and Silence*: "The entire history of women's struggle for self-determination has been muffled in silence over and over. One serious cultural obstacle encountered by any feminist writer is that each feminist work has tended to be received as if it emerged from nowhere" (11). A decade later, Trinh T. Minh-ha expands this idea to emphasize the importance of women writers of color, who should work towards "re-establishing the contact with her foremothers, so that living tradition can never congeal into fixed forms, so that life keeps on nurturing life, so that what is understood as the Past continues to provide the link for the Present and the Future" (148–49). Ng's novel emerges from these feminist foremothers, and also from her fellow Chinese American novelists. Fae Myenne Ng, whom Celeste Ng cites in her *Salon* list of Chinese American women writers to read, is one such literary foremother. Fae Myenne Ng's 1993 novel *Bone*, like *Everything I Never Told You*, narrates the death of a beloved middle daughter of a Chinese American family by following her family backward into their troubled past. *Bone*'s narrator, Leila, reflects at one point that her parents ensure that the death of her sister is cloaked in familial silence: "Don't tell this and don't tell that . . . we graduated from keeping their secrets to keeping our own" (109). Although the two novels have very different narrative structures—*Bone* moves back in time with each chapter, all in first person, while *Everything I Never Told You* shifts from past to present through omniscient narration—they share a thematic concern with the past as the root of the tragic and never fully explained death of a young girl. Furthermore, both novels share a connection back to Kingston and her desire to plunge, through writing, into a past the family would prefer to forget.

The connection between Celeste Ng and Maxine Hong Kingston appears from the very beginning, as both novels start with the story of a Chinese woman from the past, drowning and condemned to silence. *The Woman Warrior*'s first line, "'You must not tell anyone,' my mother said, 'What I am about to tell you,'" (Kingston 3) entices the reader into an intimate conversation with the promise that a "forbidden, dirty, exciting, and power-fully important" tidbit is about to follow (Parrott 375). While drawing us in to hear more, it simultaneously enforces the code of silence and emphasizes the risks Kingston takes in the very act of speaking to us through the text. The mother's forbidden story concerns Kingston's aunt, who became pregnant out of wedlock and was tormented and outcast until she drowned herself and her newborn in the town well. Kingston establishes her memoir as an act of undoing the mandated silencing of her aunt's story: "But there is more to this silence: they want me to participate in her punishment. And I have" (16). Her family's refusal to speak leaves Kingston with no access to the truth, and so she invents several possible versions of the aunt's story, including that she is either seductress to her lover or unwilling victim to her rapist (or both). As the author, Kingston thus fills silences with more stories than necessary, cre-ating myriad possible truths. As Jill Parrott observes, "This tension between what is spoken/not spoken, written/not written, given power/powerless is the ultimate conflict of the novel because it highlights the power differentials of the characters' linguistic interactions" (380). Parrott details the many ways the women in the book are silenced—via force, self-restraint, or translation of one narrative in exclusion of others—all connecting language to systems of power. As she notes, both silencing another and choosing silence oneself can create power imbalances.

The undoing of these silences, both empowering and otherwise, proves complicated. The dead cannot speak, and so despite Kingston's best inten-tions, she can only speak for her aunt, not with her. As King-Kok Cheung has observed, Kingston thus undoes not her aunt's silence but her own: "in fact, her aunt—who could not possibly inhabit all these versions—remains inescapably silent. This haunting silence is precisely what gives wings to the niece's imagination, allowing Maxine to test her own power to talk story and to play with different identities" (Cheung 85). Cheung discusses at length how Kingston undermines objective reality by weaving together autobiog-raphy and fiction,[2] creating a world where a writer can shape reality rather than being indebted to it. As Kingston told interviewer Alexis Cheung, she endeavors to show through her memoir that "there isn't a wall between fiction and nonfiction—that the borders and the margins are very wide—and that we could live in that wide border, that wide margin" ("I Can Write My Shadow"). This is not only an artistic statement but a political one about removing boundaries that keep so many writers, past and present, silenced. As Michelle Tokarczyk observes, "it is a form uniquely suited to the story and language of a working-class ethnic woman writer, a writer who is constantly crossing cultures and socioeconomic groups, who is keenly aware of her marginal status and also keenly aware of herself as a member of various communities" (54). Although Kingston cannot speak for her aunt with complete accuracy, her awareness of her own intersectional position and the fluid genre of her writing enables her to give voice to an experience likely to resonate widely.

One of Kingston's most inclusive narrative techniques is her depiction of not only her own silencing but her culpability in silencing others; throughout the memoir she crosses boundaries between oppressor and oppressed. In *The Woman Warrior*'s final chapter, Kingston returns to her own childhood and excoriates her younger self for abusing an even quieter Chinese girl in an attempt to make her speak. Young Maxine unwittingly uses the defense mechanism of projection,[3] abusing someone else to exorcise the silence she demonizes in herself. Speaking of this episode with Alexis Cheung forty years later, Kingston notes, "Remember when the narrator is bullying the other girl? She says to her, "Just say 'ow.' Just say anything, just make a sound." I guess that's the first step: make a sound. I think for everybody that just being able to speak up is a bravery, which they have to learn" ("I Can Write My Shadow"). In writing about this incident from her childhood, Kingston makes her shameful act public and published, thereby belatedly punishing herself for its commission. This section of the memoir emphasizes the narrator through its obsessive use of "I," focusing the narration entirely on the author/perpetrator's cruelty rather than the victim's suffering. Maxine torments the girl so extensively she brings herself to tears, yet her relentless verbal assault continues unabated: "I couldn't stop crying and talking at the same time" (181). The girl manages to defy her tormentor by maintaining her silence in the face of bribery, pleading, and both physical and mental abuse. Shortly before the girl's sister comes to her rescue, Maxine simultaneously begs her victim to speak and, in a reflection of the novel's opening lines, prohibits her from doing so: "Don't you dare tell anyone I've been bad to you. Talk. Please talk" (181). In demanding both silence and speech, she insists that the girl occupy the impossible double position she herself does. In keeping with the multitudes-containing contradictions of the text, Kingston associates the imposition of silence with both cultures at different times: "I knew the silence had to do with being a Chinese girl," (166), she says at one point, only to mention later that, "Normal Chinese women's voices are strong and bossy. We American-Chinese girls had to whisper to make ourselves American-feminine" (172). As Patti L. Duncan puts it, Kingston uses these contradictions to interrogate any imposed essentialism: "For Kingston, Chinese identity is neither static nor essential . . . Is silence inherently Chinese? Is speech?" (37). Neither is always true, but Kingston perceives that both Chinese and American cultures, at different times and in different ways, silence women. As a young girl, she felt the pressures of silence to be omnipresent, and she only finds herself able to defeat them, far later, through writing.

Nearly a half-century later, Kingston has found other ways to make her voice heard. If *Woman Warrior* remains her best-known work, it is far from her only success, as she has nine works of varying genres (novels, poetry, published lectures, etc.) to her name. As she told Angels Carabí in an interview, writing is a consistent and often painful act of undoing enforced silences: "I think that this is a theme in the women's writing: 'how can I break silence.' Also there are great taboos in the tribe, family secrets, skeletons in a closet. Then there is the dilemma for the writer: 'I am a writer, I am a person who 'must' tell.' There is the struggle of how to find the voice when everyone conspires and orders you to put all these things away" (143). Beyond this continual fight to tell suppressed stories, Kingston has worked to help others find their own voices; she served as a writing teacher for veterans with post-traumatic stress disorder (PTSD), editing an anthology of their work entitled *Veterans of War, Veterans of Peace.* She also volunteered as a feminist/pacifist activist with Code Pink, arrested for protesting the invasion of Iraq; never without a sense of humor and an author's eye, "she compared the participants' arrest, in which each middle-aged woman completely dressed in pink was escorted to the wagon by a somewhat reluctant officer, to a bad high school dance" (Tokarczyk 94). Through her power with words, Kingston transformed the veterans' pain into prose and her own arrest into comedy. She sought out activities that would help to amplify the voices of others, speaking with them rather than for them.

In her most recent book, *I Love a Broad Margin to My Life*, Kingston returns to the memoir form, again telling "family secrets." She begins the book by calling writing "this well-deep outpouring" (4), harkening back to the well at the beginning of her first book. She physically returns to that same well on a trip to China, and drinks from the waters that were once contaminated by her ancestress, a kind of ritual cleansing. As Audrey Ng describes it, this is part of her process of shifting her narrative from war to peace: "this ritual of immersion and blessing is a gentle reversal of her aunt's deliberate contamination of the village well by throwing herself into it; the same water that fostered the dispersal of No Name Woman's body becomes the occasion of communal healing and reconciliation" (162). If writing is a "well-deep outpouring," then the sharing of well-water suggests an end to the imposition of secrecy and a move towards sharing family history. At the conclusion of her lyrical memoir, Kingston suggests her task is complete by pledging to "Become reader of the world, no more writer of it" (221). She has kept this promise so far, in a sense: She works only on a book to be published 100 years after her death, which is, as she told Alexis Cheung, "a fact that frees her." She explains that in her earlier writing she had felt "almost a duty to be uplifting," but now, she transcends even that self-silencing: "I can put my negative emotions in . . . I can write my shadow."

Perhaps she has helped other writers who follow her to free themselves from this sense of obligation to optimism. Celeste Ng might also be described as a shadow-writer, exposing the dark traumas underlying seemingly average family lives. While Kingston's protagonist is (mostly) the author, and thus gains a literary voice of her own, Ng is quite separate from her protagonist, whose silence lasts until and beyond her death. As Chingyen Yang Mayer discusses, both Kingston and her followers break their familial norms of Confucianism by breaking their familial silences: "Their telling of forbidden stories is not only a powerful act of disruption and resistance to dominant cultural, racial and sexual discourses, but also an assertion of their Chinese American female identities" (226). Writing in the present but setting her novel in the same time period as *The Woman Warrior*, Ng recreates the cultural climate that gave rise to Kingston's masterpiece. *Everything I Never Told You* emphasizes the insurmountable challenges of the 1970s that silenced her protagonist's voice forever, while simultaneously calling on her present-day readership to fight for all those oppressed by our long-standing and still extant hegemonic silencing.

CELESTE NG'S INTERSECTIONAL IDENTITIES

Intersectionality, defined in the Introduction as the study of the "matrix of dominations" that can impact any individual's life, is critical in understanding the silences of Ng's novel (Collins 18). Every major character is marginalized in one or more ways: the two Lee males are subjected to racism from being visibly Chinese; the father's ostracization is compounded by his family's poverty; the White mother confronts repeated sexism in the workplace; and the two daughters, Lydia and Hannah, are arguably the most silenced through their identities as Chinese and female. Even the one White male character in the book, their neighbor, Jack, is otherized by his homosexuality, a secret he must guard assiduously in 1970s suburbia. As Crystal Parikh explains, the death of Lydia, the Lee's "perfect child," "interrupts a liberal narrative that centers on middle-class families in 'middle America' (e.g., the novel is set in Middlewood, Ohio) in which all sorts of subjects (women, racial minorities, immigrants, queer folks) are supposed to progressively integrate as full and equal citizens, assimilating to the norms of a possessive, autonomous individualism" (246). The range of characters' intersectional identities extends this disruption beyond Lydia; her death is only one symptom of the fragmentation Ng sees in middle America and will employ as the focus of her subsequent novel, *Little Fires Everywhere*. Through a matrix of identities, Ng demonstrates that the problem of silencing can't be confined to race or gender inequities; rather, it is both/and, merging and crystalizing in Lydia and Hannah, who, like their creator, confront both racism and sexism. In the death of the older sister and metaphorical rebirth of the younger, Ng's novel details the anguish of a life lived in secrecy, and how only its destruction can lead to renewal for the family left behind.

While the novel's plot details the impacts of this silencing, its causes are more complex and understated. As a *Guardian* article states of Ng's second novel, "The surface may appear smooth but lurking problems (race, class) will eventually rise; disruption is required for truths to be revealed" (Laity). Early in *Everything I Never Told You*, Ng suggests that the origins of silence lie not only in the characters' historical moments but in how the separate psychologies and mutual interactions of the Lee parents, Marilyn and James, respond to the prejudices of their times. She concisely summarizes what she will gradually unravel and reveal by beginning with the roots of the family story, which occurred: "because of Lydia's mother and father, because of her mother's and father's mothers and fathers. Because long ago, her mother had gone missing, and her father had brought her home. Because, more than anything, her mother had wanted to stand out; because more than anything, her father had wanted to blend in. Because those things had been impossible" (25).[4] In wanting to "stand out" and "blend in," Marilyn and James struggle with the silence imposed on them via misogyny and racism, respectively. Both are denied a voice in the public sphere, but this silence impacts each of them psychologically and relationally as well. Being forced into silence repeatedly, hegemonically, is problematic enough; but, the novel argues, this enforced silence corrupts our most intimate relationships, beginning with marriage and branching outward into offspring. Once James and Marilyn resign themselves to their own silences, they each separately elect Lydia to gain a voice on their vicarious behalf. When the Lees are in college in the 1950s, the idea of professional and social acceptance for minorities seems impossible; by the time Lydia is growing up in the 1970s, both erroneously believe their Chinese daughter will have all the opportunities they lacked. Lydia drowns, however, not in societal rejection but in her parents' impossible expectations and failure to communicate sufficiently for her to break through them.

Ng's temporal location in 2014 provides the final narrative reframing. The omniscient narrator is not technically Ng but is a voice from a later age, capable of bearing witness to the characters' future lives. The dynamic of these multiple narrative perspectives emphasizes how the silencing of the past can inhibit speech and agency for generations to come. Little has changed even in these turbulent decades, and, the novel suggests, if we do not break our own culturally imposed silences, little will.

PAPER SONS AND CHINATOWN COWBOYS

Writing in the 1970s, the authors of *Aiiieeeee! An Anthology of Asian-American Writers*, describe the climate for Asian Americans that would have been all too familiar to the Lee family. *Aiiieeeee!* was the first major collection of Asian American writing; notably, its editors were all Asian men, and only four of the fourteen collected authors are women, so the selections skew masculine. In their 1973 preface, Chin et al. state that "Seven generations of suppression under legislative racism and euphemized white racist love have left today's Asian-Americans in a state of self-contempt, self-rejection, and disintegration" (xii). The authors repeat "seven generations" multiple times, underscoring that it was not the presence of Asian Americans that was new to the country but merely the acknowledgment of their achievements. The collection is an attempt to grant retroactive recognition and, thus, combat the described self-loathing. They go on to state: "This myth of being either/ or and the equally goofy concept of the dual personality haunted our lobes while our rejection by both Asia and white America proved we were neither one nor the other" (xii). Here the authors harken back to W.E.B. Du Bois's well-known concept of double-consciousness from the turn of the twentieth century, while both the general tone and the specific word "goofy" express outrage that so little has changed over time. Bewildering and obsolete though such double-consciousness may have seemed by the 1970s, it is very much the world James Lee inherits, both on a cultural and personal level.

James's parents live a life built on secrets. Their very existence must be kept hidden, because the Chinese Exclusion Acts rendered immigration from China effectively illegal from 1882 to 1943. As Ng puts it, the United States government banned Chinese immigration because they feared "the molten mixture was becoming a shade too yellow" in the melting pot (40). As a result, "The *coolies* had to find other means to reach the land where all men were created equal" (40). Ng neatly emphasizes the contrast between America's ideals and praxis in these lines: an alleged melting pot can still be "too yellow," and Americans are "created equal," yet still disparaged for their race and class as "coolies." As history has proven, immigration cannot be easily blocked by prejudice, or laws, or walls. Because children of legal immigrants could enter the United States, the Chinese resourcefully created a system of "paper sons," in which Chinese Americans would falsely claim children from back home who were then granted legal entry. This pragmatic work-around took a lasting psychological toll, however: "the lives of all those paper sons were fragile and easily torn. Everyone's name was false" (Ng 41). Maxine Hong Kingston similarly grew up with the threat that breaking silence could mean deportation for paper sons: "There were secrets never to be said in front of the ghosts, immigration secrets whose telling could get us sent back to China" (*Woman Warrior* 183). In Fae Myenne Ng's *Bone*, the narrator attempts to sift through family documents and observes, "I'm the stepdaughter of a paper son and I've inherited this whole suitcase of lies" (58). The undermining of identity for paper sons in each book perpetuates both racial shame and a systemic secrecy. Eventually the desire to avoid detection and deportation caused the Chinese to become extolled as a so-called "model minority"; silence that began as a survival tactic was lauded as a virtue.

Increasingly Chinese Americans found this alleged docility culturally reinforced by their new country. As Chin et al. describe it, immigrants became "'Chinese-American' in the stereotypical sense of the good, loyal, obedient, passive, law-abiding, cultured sense of the word" (*Aiiieeeee!* xiv). Families like James's benefited from this perception; impoverished, the Lees obtain menial labor jobs at an exclusive boarding school, with free tuition and thus upward mobility for James, because the employers believe the Chinese work hard and stay quiet. Being quiet, however, comes at a cost. Frank Chin's 1972 essay "Confessions of a Chinatown Cowboy" explicitly connects the model minority concept to enforced silences, explaining that speaking either English or Chinese could isolate and mark you, so silence became preferable. Furthermore, Chin saw this silencing as specifically gendered: "Language as it was known in the world [of Chinatown] was emasculating, sissy stuff" (68). The language he uses attempts to contradict this stereotype by being explicitly masculine: "Ride with this Chinatown cowboy a bit while I run off to rustle strange words and maverick up a language to write this mess in" (Chin 71).[5] The stereotype of Asian men as emasculated lingers, however, as Jinqui Ling summarizes: "The traditional western concept of masculinity—which values men as embodiments of civilization, rationality, and aggressiveness and devalues women as embodiments of primitiveness, emotion, and passivity . . . was extended to account for the West's sense of economic and political superiority over Asia by projecting the latter as a diametrically opposed feminine Other" (314). Ling, building from Edward Said's *Orientalism*,[6] frames the emasculation of Asians as a tool of postcolonial hegemony. Longing to achieve assertiveness and visibility in the face of this persistent stereotyping, James follows in Chin's footsteps, using cowboys to embody his ego ideal: Western and masculine; strong and silent.

Even teaching a course on cowboys at Harvard does not allow James to fit in, however, and without ever having left the United States he continues to view himself as an outsider. He seeks belonging in Marilyn, whom he misperceives as someone who never feels out of place, and whose love makes him feel "as if America herself was taking him in" (45).[7] Their relationship could offer him a way to leave the lonely cowboy identity behind and share his fears with a sympathetic partner as they ride off into the sunset. The zeitgeist of the era renders such a happy ending impossible, however. Their relationship is shrouded in secrecy from the beginning, as Marilyn starts as James's student, becomes unexpectedly pregnant before she graduates, and marries him in a quick and quiet courthouse ceremony. Furthermore, their marriage is illegal in half of the country in 1958; only a few decades before that, a White woman could lose her citizenship for marrying an Asian man. Imbued with this societal sense of shame, the couple commences their marriage with a willful obfuscation of all that came before, vowing to "let the past drift away, to stop asking questions, to look forward from then on, never back" (49). Silences once made prove challenging to undo, and the couple becomes slowly but inexorably incapable of discussing matters quite relevant to their present: specifically, their traumas in combatting racism and sexism, respectively. Although Marilyn has suffered from prejudice as well, James cannot confide in her about his childhood struggles, terrified that Marilyn will come to see him "as he had always seen himself: a scrawny outcast, feeding on scraps, reciting his lines and trying to pass. An imposter" (48). James's words show a complex picture of his fears, indicating in turn his anxieties about being emasculated, poor, "passing," and, finally, an "imposter." The "Imposter Phenomenon," a persistent feeling of inadequacy unaltered by verifiable success, first appeared in publication in 1978, just after the time when the novel ends (Clance and Imes). Although Drs. Pauline Clance and Suzanne Imes focused this initial study on "high achieving women" like themselves, the concept was later expanded to include people of color and those of working-class backgrounds—two categories that apply to James (Clance and Imes). While aspiring to the cowboy ideal, James remains an insubstantial paper son in his own perception.

James copes with his feelings of inadequacy by projecting them onto others—most notably his own son. Predating the "personality rating," Nathan Lee's introversion and awkwardness do not prevent him from receiving a Harvard acceptance letter; yet James measures him against a standard of masculinity rather than one of academic success, ruefully observing that his awkward son, "legs twisted, stacking the toes of one foot atop the other—reminded him of himself" (88). He wants more for Nath, but even in his imagination he can only see his son as a sidekick to their White neighbor, Jack, fantasizing about the games they might play: "Jack as the captain and Nath as the first mate. Sheriff and deputy. Batman and Robin" (89). In each iteration, the White male plays the dominant role, and his Chinese son the subordinate one. When young Nath is bullied in the pool, James empathizes but cannot break the habit of silence enough to reveal his own past. Longing to share with Nath his own similar experiences of childhood torment but simultaneously wishing "to shake his son, to slap him," James chooses an unpleasant middle ground of quiet contempt (92). James, much like Kingston's younger avatar, desperately wants to destroy the racially configured weakness he loathes in himself by projecting it onto another. Refusing to speak of his own experiences with prejudice reinforces the toxic culture of silence, leaving it to the next generation as a contaminated inheritance.

Alienated from his family and devastated by Lydia's death, James seeks to enhance his injured sense of self-worth through an affair with his teaching assistant, Louisa. In doing so, James is arguably combatting the stereotype of the emasculated Chinese male that Frank Chin decried, noting that "the evil of the evil Dr. Fu Manchu was not sexual but homosexual" (95). Choosing Louisa is also a way for James to excoriate himself for the perceived audacity of believing that a White woman could love him, and to convince himself that he should have married someone Chinese. Louisa is the anti-Marilyn not only racially, however, but also in her conformity to gender roles; Marilyn observes her timidity and thinks she is "as far from me . . . as a girl could be" (215). She embodies the feminine stereotype of cooking—one that is anathema to Marilyn—wooing James with Chinese steamed buns redolent of his childhood. James accepts this gift from Louisa orally, both by consuming them and naming them aloud, *char siu bau*, which become the first Chinese words he has spoken in forty years. James's self-silencing was profound enough that he willfully lost access to his own first language. The verbal expression of Chinese seems to thrust him from his infantilized state, and his ensuing sex with Louisa is aggressive, beginning when he shoves her down rather than waiting for her to embrace him. Reclaiming language induces potency, but this fleetingly macho behavior empowers the man while wounding the women in his life, as it so often does. Frank Chin observed that the Chinese in the 1970s were forced into a feminine role by White patriarchy: "America has locked the whole race into the same housewife stereotype women are running out of town" ("Confessions" 100). In this scene, James's brief liberation appears to be a zero-sum game, for while his virility subverts the emasculation of the Chinese, his hunger for a quiet woman who cooks confirms the inescapability of that very housewife stereotype for Marilyn.

FROM CROCKER TO DOCTOR

Marilyn's ambition is both a product of her natural intelligence and an attempt to make her voice heard in a patriarchal culture that systematically silences women. Marilyn spent her childhood watching her own mother aspiring to nothing more than exemplifying the Virginian ideal homemaker in the 1930s and losing her husband nonetheless: "So they called it *keeping house* for a reason, Marilyn thought. Sometimes it did run away" (28). Marilyn's mother never mentions her father again, beginning the cycle of silence. When she dies, she leaves another lacuna, another unspoken narrative, for Marilyn perceives that she "had planned on a golden, vanilla-scented life but ended up alone, trapped like a fly in this small and sad and empty house" (83). Marilyn grows up determined to be different and to make her voice heard. She chooses to become a doctor because, above all, it is that path that will separate her most definitively from all of her mother's aspirations and expectations.

Despite her considerable aptitude and ambition, however, Marilyn finds herself silenced through a series of microaggressions which, intentionally and not, keep women in their place. Although the reader receives these events out of chronological order, piecing them together reveals the impact of constant belittling on Marilyn's sense of identity. In 1952, the principal denies her request to take shop instead of her mother's Home Economics class because her beauty would prove too distracting to all her male classmates. In 1955, she tells her Radcliffe advisor she wants to be a doctor and is quickly dismissed with a chuckle and the suggestion that she pursue nursing instead. In 1966, she asks her husband's scientist colleague about working in his lab to restart her career, but he, too, laughs off her offer as unsuitable for a wife and mother. In fact, the scientist had interpreted Marilyn's initial request as flirtation, evidently finding it more plausible that a married woman would seek an affair than lab work. Each of these not-so-slight slights, familiar to many women then and now, accumulate to silence Marilyn and her career ambitions.

Marilyn continues to pursue her dream of becoming a doctor until the opposing voices simply become overpowering. It is not as if women doctors were entirely unheard of in her time, even within the pages of this novel.[8] My students, therefore, often cannot comprehend why Marilyn takes the drastic action of abandoning her family to finish her degree in another town, rather than openly stating her ambitions and enlisting their support. The block for Marilyn is not pragmatic, however, but psychological, for she knows that she and nearly everyone around her hears the word "doctor" and "still thought—would forever think—*man*" (143). She cannot envision a world where a mother of multiple children could be a doctor as well.[9] This is not to say that such a thing is easy, even today; we need only look to the volume of research written on the motherhood wage gap, Anne-Marie Slaughter's infamous *Atlantic* article on why women still can't have it all, or a *Guardian* report from 2018 observing, "As a culture and a profession, medicine continues to systematically disadvantage women physicians at every stage of their careers" (Poorman). What is challenging now, however, was impossible for Marilyn by the age of 40 in the late 1970s. Adrienne Rich describes the culture of the time in her 1976 essay tellingly titled, "Motherhood in Bondage": "all women are seen primarily as mothers; all mothers are expected to experience motherhood unambivalently and in accordance with patriarchal values; and the 'nonmothering' woman is seen as deviant" (196). This is evident in the novel through the town's disparagement of Dr. Wolff, a single mother who lets her son run as wild as their bestial surname suggests. The collective opprobrium she faces emphasizes that women are expected not only to procreate but to define themselves through motherhood. Rich elaborated on this theme in 1978: "The unmarried or childless woman may be more acceptable today than when she was perceived as so threatening that she was burned as a witch. But the socialization of every girl toward heterosexual romance and childbearing is still probably the most intense socialization practiced by society as a whole" (264). Despite the progress evident in legal gay marriage and increasingly open views of gender identity, this statement arguably holds true today.

Not only was Marilyn a product of gender constructions of her time, however, but she was subjected to the hegemonic culture pervading her household. Early in her relationship with James, Marilyn reveals only one piece of information about her mother: "Betty Crocker is her personal goddess" (47). Although James notes that this "sounded like a secret, something she had kept hidden and now deliberately, trustingly, revealed" (47), he does not know why. Even in this intimate moment of trust, Marilyn chooses not to explain why this seemingly innocuous statement provides confidential information, or how her mother's housekeeping dreams have shaped her own goals in contradistinction. Instead, she remains silently haunted by her mother's Betty Crocker cookbook, which seems to serve up relentless patriarchy along with tips on potatoes and pie crust. Ng found the following advice about eggs, which she thematically weaves throughout the novel, in her mother's actual, slightly later but similarly retrograde edition of the cookbook: "it behooves a good wife to know how to make an egg behave in six basic ways" (83). Neatly packaged in a cookbook, there is the man who knows what he likes; and there is the woman, caught between "behoove" and "behave." Implicitly, a woman's role is to beat eggs, whether chicken or ovarian, into meek submission for male enjoyment. Marilyn can rebel against this edict, and she does. But being doctor and mother of three is simply further than she can imagine herself outside the confines of that cookbook.

Once a third pregnancy thwarts her desperate flight to become a doctor, Marilyn's life goals inarguably have been compromised by her own eggs. Brygida Gasztold points out the irony of the fact that despite her interest in both medical matters and feminist objectives, Marilyn "fails to benefit from another gain of the women's lib movement—access to reliable oral contraception . . . in Marilyn's case life has written its own script" (74). Perhaps this, too, is a consequence of silence: shame around birth control has long kept women from discussing it openly to each other, or to their medical providers, especially when those providers were uniformly male. If so, this silence begets others when Marilyn's 1966 disappearance in pursuit of a medical career proves to be the foundational but unspoken trauma for the entire family. In fact, her absence "suffused them so deeply it could never wash out" precisely because "the family has never spoken of it" (124, 102). Marilyn's absence is debilitating, but the family's attempted erasure of it leaves the repressed poised to return with a vengeance, as it inevitably does. The same silence envelopes Lydia's drowning: "Don't talk about Lydia. Don't talk about the lake. Don't ask questions" (106). This constant silencing, psychologically traumatic in any event, exacerbates the gendered silencing Marilyn has been subjected to her entire life.

After abandoning her desired medical career, Marilyn invests herself in fostering Lydia's undesired one, vowing she would "help Lydia do everything she was capable of" (147). But which *she* does the sentence imply: Marilyn or Lydia? Marilyn's goals and aspirations become entirely rooted in her daughter, meaning they have unwittingly become those of her own mother.[10] Her decision to head towards a new life simply turns her back towards the one she fled, as she resolves to dedicate herself wholeheartedly to mothering Lydia: "sheltering her, the way you tended a prize rose: helping it grow, propping it with stakes, arching each stem toward perfection" (147). Though her metaphor may be botanical, Marilyn is still forcing her "egg" to behave. Her feminist ambitions are silenced, sent back to the kitchen.

GIRLHOODS AMONG GHOSTS

Lydia, both Chinese and female, is doubly impacted by the racism and sexism of the world around her. Poet and activist Audre Lorde spoke eloquently about being a woman of color during this time at the 1977 Modern Language Association (MLA) convention: "I am not only a casualty, I am also a warrior. What are the words you do not have yet? What do you need to say? What are the tyrannies you swallow day by day and attempt to make your own, until you will sicken and die of them, still in silence?" (41). For, she tells her audience, "My silences had not protected me. Your silence will not protect you" (41). Lydia's parents hold out hope that her adolescence in the 1970s will prove more auspicious than theirs several decades before, but as Lorde makes clear, women of color were still suffering from the impositions of silence at this time. Arguably, the inclination towards suppression of overt racism in the present day has not entirely changed matters, for Ng notes that all of the micro- and macroaggressions in the book, "actually happened at some point to me, my family, or others I know personally" (Laity). In revealing them through her novel, Ng counters the common narrative that such prejudice is all in the past.

The "tyrannies" that Lydia must "swallow day by day" are both instigated and endlessly reinforced by her parents' own silences. Marilyn's absence and return ensnares Lydia in the unspoken threat that if she does not fulfill her mother's medical ambitions, Marilyn will once again leave the family. This causes Lydia's unwavering dedication to her childhood promise that, if her mother does return, "she would do everything her mother told her"—an impossibly self-sacrificing pledge that, like Lydia herself, never has the chance to grow or change with maturity (137). Thus both mother and daughter remain silent about their own separate ambitions, communicating only through promises subtly extracted and desperately kept. Marilyn pushes Lydia's science career with an unintentionally disingenuous preface: "'Only if you want to.' She meant it, every time, but she did not realize she was holding her breath" (159). This physical cue conveys what her words do not, and Lydia pays attention, aware that only once she concedes to each new academic challenge will Marilyn take her next life-sustaining breath. Assiduously fulfilling her mother's every expectation sets her apart, thereby thwarting her father's desperate desire for her to fit in. Like him, she is separated by her physical appearance, for "even with blue eyes, she could not pretend she blended in" (192),[11] instead finding herself taunted and haunted by her playmates' whispered racial slurs and gestures. Lydia's biracial appearance parallels the way she is divided between both parents, leaving her further fractured. Being a part of the only Asian family in her town, coupled with being the only girl taking college-level science courses, however reluctantly, makes it impossible to gain an identity of her own; while "one or the other might be overcome," the combination proves insurmountable (227). The pressure of fulfilling both parents' failed ambitions as attempted compensation for the prejudices they have suffered compounds Lydia's struggles to define her own identity against those same prejudices.

As a result, Lydia becomes permanently silenced from both sides. After her death, James seeks answers from her autopsy report but can only understand enough to imagine the details as metaphors. Envisioning her alveoli as sugar-coated, her lungs like impressionable dough, her skin peeling like a glove, can help him imagine his daughter's inner being only in the most literal sense.[12] Marilyn's attempt to gain access to Lydia's internal life takes a slightly different form; eschewing autopsy reports she instead seeks answers in her daughter's diaries. To her disappointment Lydia has left them all completely blank, bequeathing her mother nothing but "page after page of visible, obstinate silence" (74). 1966, the year the empty diaries begin, is also the year Marilyn temporarily left her family; during that period, Lydia would watch, fittingly, *I've Got a Secret* on TV, as she "stared glassy-eyed at the screen in silence" (130). The family's refusal to speak of the trauma of the mother's absence is a kind of corpse that is never autopsied, and from that moment on, Lydia's secrets and silences becomes so absolute that she has nothing to say, even in writing, even to herself.

Instead, Lydia hides behind a humorless smile, the false self she presents to the world to conceal the damage inflicted by the weight of her family's collapsed dreams.[13] In the Lee family, gifts are "less presents than unsubtle hints," and James uses them to pressure Lydia to maintain a smile that serves as the semblance of social acceptance, though not its harbinger (173). The locket he gives to Lydia comes with a caveat, requiring her promise that she will smile whenever she looks at it. Ironically, the photo James places in the locket commemorates a school dance so miserable that Lydia isn't even smiling in the picture. She realizes the locket is a noose posing as a memento: "a string around her finger, although this lay around her neck" (228). Even less subtle is James's gift of a book, *How to Win Friends and Influence People*, which, like Marilyn's loathed cookbook, Ng quotes verbatim, highlighting real-life societally enforced constructions of behavior: "Don't criticize, condemn, or complain" and "Force yourself to smile" (178, 181). This book inspires the same antipathetic reaction in Lydia that the cookbook did in her mother, and in a quiet moment of rebellion, she refuses to smile for the camera as instructed and expected. Both her resistance and remaining life are brief, however, and Hannah describes her expression in a birthday photo taken shortly before her death as "terrifying": "the smile was too wide, too bright, cheery and wide-toothed and fake" (237). In the wake of her disappearance, this image receives publication and public circulation; Lydia's least genuine self becomes her photographic epitaph.

Lydia's death does not end all the long-held familial silences, but it does generate critical moments of empathy in each of the characters. In the wake of her loss, James has an epiphany about his wife, realizing that "different," a concept he had so feared, "had been different for Marilyn" (251). Preparing to leave his wife, he finds himself suddenly capable of imagining their life from her perspective: "Triply sequestered by house and dead-end street and tiny college town, her hands soft and uncalloused but idle. The intricate gears of her mind ticking silently at no one" (251). James focuses on Marilyn's mind, which he has long overlooked, and her hands, contrasting his own wish to keep them comfortably smooth with Marilyn's desire for a doctor's callouses. While these lines show a critical moment of understanding, the words are Ng's, not James's, and the narrator observes that he will never achieve their articulation: "James will struggle to piece words to this feeling, and he will never quite manage to say, even just to himself, what he really means" (252). Similarly, Marilyn recalls their wedding empathically through James's perspective, remembering how casually she told her new husband that her mother disapproved of his race and comprehending the message's near-physical impact only years later: "those words had haunted James. How they must have wound around his heart, binding tighter over the years, slicing into the flesh" (213). She, too, keeps these feelings silent, speaking to James only in her mind: *"I would marry you a hundred times if it gave us Lydia"* (213). The beginning of this line promises a romantic conclusion that dissipates at the sadly significant "if": a reminder that her love for James is contingent upon its physical and now deceased product.

Though these empathic moments prove incommunicable, both parents effectively demonstrate empathy for their youngest daughter, Hannah, in the aftermath of Lydia's death. Throughout most of the novel, Hannah is so silent as to be ignored even by the text itself; she appears rarely, and when she does, it is almost an absent presence: "Hannah's body knows all the secrets of silence," or "her silence tells him she is listening" (103, 123). Even devastating information about Hannah appears as the narrator's parenthetical aside, as when we learn that Hannah is tucked in the attic, "where things that were not wanted were kept," and that for years Marilyn forgets to set a place at the table for the third, unwanted child (161). Relegated to vacant spaces and excerpted from family meals, Hannah exists only in the margins. The boundaries shift after Lydia's death, however, and the narration turns to the forgotten sister in the end. Hannah successfully resists the patriarchal smile requirement both because she has not yet been acculturated to do otherwise and because shortly before dying Lydia advised her little sister to smile only for herself, not others. Hannah seems to learn this lesson and her subsequent smiles are not for show. Her slight compassionate smile to Jack when she recognizes and identifies with his unexpressed, unrequited love for her brother appears genuine. In the end, Hannah giggles with glee as her father plays with her, seemingly for the first time, and Marilyn gives her a goodnight kiss on the head, punctuating a lifetime of starvation for physical contact. The final words of the novel refer to Hannah, from Nath's perspective: "He doesn't want to dive underwater and lose sight of her face" (292). The forgotten child is in turn heard, touched, and seen by each surviving family member. She will not be the silenced drowned girl, for she remains firmly on land. Although she will, like Lydia, face both racism and misogyny, she may not suffer as severely from the traumas of the past. And perhaps, if the reader pays attention to the omniscient narrator, neither will we.

FUTURE OMNISCIENT

The very first sentences of the novel both reveal the novel's major plotline and distance the knowing narrator from the unsuspecting characters: "Lydia is dead. But they don't know this yet" (1). Ng states that at first she was reluctant to use the omniscient narrator ("because I'm not Dickens, and the omniscient narrator is sort of like playing god"), which she sees as gendered: "I always think of Dickens's narrator as being a man" ("Politics and Prose," 28:06, 29:22). She chose to use the technique in the end, however, because "I wanted the reader always to be able to see a little farther than the characters could" (28:38). In the *New York Times Book Review*, Eliot Holt describes Ng's technique as distinct from the traditional Dickensian version of "narrators who intrude to remind the reader how little the characters know" (Holt). Ng, he claims, demonstrates an updated version, the "return of omniscience": "The old metaphor for omniscience was 'author as God,' but in our largely secular digital age, authorial divinity could be replaced by a new analogy: author as smartphone . . . Perhaps the return of omniscient narrators reflects the sense we all have, as internet users, of access to unlimited knowledge" (Holt). Ng's first two novels, however, are set in eras before the omniscience of Google, which limits both the characters' access to knowledge and to other people.[14] The novel's particular sense of isolation and despair might be ameliorated in our current age, which, for all its flaws, offers myriad alternatives to silence. What kind of empowerment might have been available to Jack if he had had the "It Gets Better" campaign for gay youth, or to Lydia if she had seen Tatyana Fazlalizadeh's "Stop Telling Women to Smile" activist art project, or to Marilyn if she had stumbled upon the website "500 Women Scientists," or to all the characters if the #Metoo movement had alerted them to the dangers of silence and the power of breaking it? While Ng's omniscient narrator may have the limitless knowledge of the internet, her characters suffer from a markedly circumscribed range of vision.

The novel calls attention to the characters' limited perspectives through one of its few significant intertexts: Faulkner's *The Sound and the Fury*. Written in segmented stream-of-consciousness chapters, Faulkner's novel shows a family vastly isolated from one another, each Compson brother eternally locked in his separate mental universe. It is this novel that Hannah steals from Lydia in a bid to gain her sister's attention, and despite knowing it is well above her reading level, Hannah peruses it slowly, "savoring the words like a cherry Life Saver tucked inside her cheek" (21). Hannah has taken something that is Lydia's and consumed it like a clandestine treat; in not discovering the loss, Lydia confirms Hannah's self-perception as unnoticed and insignificant. Ng emphasizes this ongoing lack of communication by reprising cherry candy at another critical moment; as in Faulkner, the reader can see this connection, but the characters cannot. During Marilyn's fateful absence, Nath takes a cherry flavored candy from Jack, seeming to be on the verge of accepting Jack himself, and perhaps even his romantic interest: "Nath slipped one of the candies into his mouth and let the sweetness seep into him and counted the freckles on Jack's cheek" (131). When Jack tries to commiserate about the loss of a parent, however, Nath, unprepared to view his mother's absence as permanent, rejects both candy and neighbor, spitting away the too-sweet cherry taste. In both scenes, the Lee siblings struggle to communicate their fears and isolation, which would be the true life saver—but they receive only saccharine cherry flavor as recompense. In order to heal, the Lee family, unlike the Compsons, will need to successfully share their private lives rather than remaining critically (fatally) divided into separate consciousnesses.

While Kingston's novel ends with the author's reclamation of her aunt's story and her own voice, Ng's ends with the drowned woman's silence broken only to the reader. Nath reflects on his sister's life and death in the final pages, realizing that he will never completely understand "what it was like, what she was thinking, everything she'd never told him" (290). The narrator, however, does know, and has already allowed the reader access to Lydia's final thoughts. In this way, Ng enacts what Vietnamese American writer Trinh T. Minh-ha recommends: "Even if the telling condemns her present life, what is more important is to (re-)tell the story as she thinks it should be told; in other words, to maintain the difference that allows (her) truth to live on" (150). The novel is a way of retelling Lydia's story, so that someone outside of the family has the opportunity to read it "as she thinks it should be told," allowing her "truth" to continue and subverting the silencing of her accidental death.

In the end, we readers alone know what none of the characters ever will: that Lydia's death was neither suicide nor murder but an accident. As Crystal Parikh describes, "Lydia's death poignantly stages the impossibility of fully controlling the direction in which our individual choices and actions lead us, as well as how they will affect those others upon whom our lives are interdependent" (245). At the moment of her death, Lydia is unaware of the impact all her secrets and silences will have on those she has left behind. Consequently, only the reader understands that her final thoughts were not despairing but hopeful: "From now on, she will do what *she* wants. Feet planted firmly on nothing, Lydia—so long enthralled by the dreams of others—could not yet imagine what that might be, but suddenly the universe glittered with possibilities" (274–275). Lydia is trying to swim, not drown, leaping into the water as an act of self-empowerment and independence. These same desires fuel Nath's fascination with astronautics, a connection reflected in Lydia's word choice in this moment: "moon," "darkness," "sky," "space," "star," and "night" (275).[15] Lydia, like most of the Lee family, is dismissive of Nath's space obsession; the author using Nath's language in Lydia's mind foreshadows Lydia's desire for a new frontier of her own. Just before her death, "she could not believe that anything was impossible" (275), which both reflects Nath's sense of wonder upon seeing the Gemini launch and suggests the gap between Lydia's knowledge and that of the readers: We understand that it is too late for Lydia to teach herself to swim. Her family has molded her to fit their own desires for so long that she never develops the ability to swim against any currents at all.

The novel does not end where it began, with Lydia's death, however. Instead, the omniscient voice takes us into the future, showing how the family will begin to heal, and closing with an image of an older Nath: "he looks at the small bump that will always mar Jack's nose and wants to trace it, gently, with his finger" (291). In this brief line, Ng implies that perhaps another silence has been lingering throughout the text; that Nath's antipathy for Jack may have been, all along, a repression of his own desire for him.[16] This conclusion emphasizes the gap between past and present by calling attention to the contrast between widely held views on sexuality then and now. In a 1976 speech to the MLA entitled, "The Lesbian Within Us," Adrienne Rich spoke of the importance of ending the silence surrounding homosexuality: "Whatever is unnamed, undepicted in images, whatever is omitted from biography, censored in collections of letters, whatever is misnamed as something else, made difficult-to-come-by, whatever is buried in the memory by the collapse of meaning under an inadequate or lying language—this will become, not merely unspoken, but unspeakable" (199). These lines aptly describe all of the silences in the book, which appear often as mere elisions rather than lies, or simple matters the characters intend to tell and yet never do. But the aggregate effect of these silences is to render not one but nearly every aspect of their lives unspeakable. Ng creates a tapestry of moments when, as Lydia considers more than once, silence seems so simple—just one lie, just one omission—but eventually the impossibility of breaking silences so long in place leads to a fractured family and, finally, to Lydia's death. The Lees' many silences extend far into the future, but the novel helps us look back to the past and consider the powerful repercussions of all the things we have not told. Radical empathy asks us to avoid silences and silencings, to both listen and raise our voices. Only by hearing the voices oppressed and suppressed can we consider how many more are yet to come to light, and what we risk if they do not.

NOTES

1. See chapter one for more on Adichie's talk.
2. See Cheung, 13, 15, 75, 77, 80.
3. Freud wrote of projection as a defense mechanism: "An internal perception is suppressed, and, instead, its content, after undergoing a certain kind of distortion,

enters consciousness in the form of an external perception" (*Standard Edition*, Vol. 12, p. 66).

4. Fae Myenne Ng's aforementioned novel *Bone* contains a similar idea of continuity from parent to child. The author writes of Ona's suicide, "The oldtimers believed that the blood came from the mother and the bones from the father. Ona was part Leon and part Mah, but neither of them could believe that Ona's unhappiness was all her own" (101).

5. Kingston and Chin had a literary feud over stereotyping; he vocally critiqued *Woman Warrior*, and she in turn made him the basis of the main character in her novels, *Tripmaster Monkey: His Fake Book* and *The Fifth Book of Peace*. For further discussion of this, see the Conclusion.

6. For example, Said writes about perceptions that "the Oriental is irrational, depraved (fallen), childlike, 'different'; thus the European is rational, virtuous, mature, 'normal.'"

7. Just as James is attracted to Marilyn because she fits in, Marilyn is drawn to James because he doesn't: "Something inside her said, He understands. What it's like to be different" (36). This is specifically racialized, as she views, in contrast, the less desirable boys with "sandy hair and ruddy skin" to be "as familiar as boiled potatoes" (37).

8. Ng introduces Marilyn to two female doctors, Dr. Greene and Dr. Wolff, demonstrating that while Marilyn's ambitions are unlikely they are not impossible.

9. This parallels Tillie Olsen's point that while women made up only "one in twelve" well-known writers in the 1950s–1960s, even fewer of those were mothers: "until very recently almost all distinguished achievement has come from childless women" (31).

10. While Marilyn parallels the stereotypical "tiger mom" in this way, Ng notes that a White woman is less likely to be labeled a "tiger mom" than the "less pejorative helicopter parent." She adds that "Marilyn's desire to become a doctor is a reaction to her particular background . . . and that felt much more specific and real and interesting than a generic 'Asian' desire to have one's child become a doctor just for the perceived prestige" ("First Fiction 2014," *Poets & Writers*).

11. This could be read as an update to Toni Morrison's *The Bluest Eye*; here, blue eyes alone don't grant inclusion, as the unfortunate Pecola Breedlove dreams.

12. Ng states that she developed this scene of a father reading his daughter's autopsy when she was in the reverse situation, as a daughter reading her father's autopsy a few years before writing the novel (*Poets & Writers*).

13. Marilyn fakes her smiles in high school as well ("It wasn't a true smile, and her dimples didn't show" [27]), emphasizing the omnipresence of smile enforcement for women.

14. *Little Fires Everywhere*, Ng's second novel, is set in the 1990s—only shortly before the internet era.

15. Ng states in a 2015 talk, "Politics and Prose," that Nath's childhood obsession with astronauts derived from her own (21:11).

16. See Yihang Ma, "Sexual Ambiguity in *Everything I Never Told You*," *Comparative Literature: East & West* (December 2018) for more on Nath's sexuality. Reading Nath as queer could further explain James's antipathy for his son, given his uneasiness about his own perceived masculinity.

Chapter Three

Journeys Within

Black Men on the Road in Song of Solomon *and* Sing, Unburied, Sing

A recent conversation captured much of the beauty of my black world.
. . . And I think I needed this vantage point before I could journey out. I
think I needed to know that I was from somewhere, that my home was as
beautiful as any other.

—Ta-Nehisi Coates, *Between the World and Me*

THE JOURNEY BEGINS: FROM THE SLAVE
SHIP TO THE LYNCHING ROPE

The authors discussed in the previous chapter depict their characters' urgent
need to delve into personal history to resolve the conflicts of the present. As I
have demonstrated, these personal narratives are often more closely entwined
with a larger network of oppression and conditioning than any individual
may realize. This chapter hopes to move us closer to radical empathy by
considering the national trauma that was slavery, and the way in which that
initial involuntary voyage continues to impact concepts of travel, freedom,
and masculinity into the present day. Terri Givens writes that if we want to
move towards a radical empathy that can address the challenges of racism in
the twenty-first century, "the first step is acknowledgement of the past" (147).
She observes that this is often counter to the American mindset: "In the US
we tend to avoid a focus on the past, and our sense of individual responsibility
makes it difficult to see the structures I have described throughout this book
that have led to injustice. Reconciliation can start with individuals, building

49

to communities and states, and ultimately to the national level" (147). With these words in mind, this chapter focuses on journeys, metaphorical and literal, to consider the ongoing impact of the past on our racial present, and how paying attention to novels by African American writers can bring us closer to a radical empathy that can shape a more just and equitable future.

To begin to trace the indelible influence of the transatlantic slave trade, we might consider a few stops of many on the literary road map. James Baldwin's 1959 essay, "Nobody Knows My Name," describes how a Black man in the North is inevitably tied to the plantation past, so that upon traveling to the South, "he sees, in effect, his ancestors, who in everything they do and are, proclaim his inescapable identity" (99). Frantz Fanon's groundbreaking 1967 book, *Black Skin, White Masks*, depicts the painful impacts of this history even more directly: "I discovered my blackness, my ethnic characteristics; and I was battered down by tom-toms, cannibalism, intellectual deficiency, fetishism, racial defects, slave-ships" (112). The slave ships at the end of the sentence, of course, were originally justified by the string of stereotypes at its start, but the stereotypes lingered long after the slave ships ceased sailing. Half a century later, a frequent phrase from *Black Skin, White Masks*, "between the world and me," became the title of Ta-Nehisi Coates' best-selling memoir.[1] In the form of a letter to his son, Coates writes of the weight of history on Black men: "It is so easy to look away, to live with the fruits of our history and to ignore the great evil done in all our names. But you and I have never truly had that luxury" (8–9). His memoir, and much of his life's work, emphasizes the importance of recalling the brutal history of slavery and its continuing impact. Contemporary poet Claudia Rankine takes a similar perspective in her poetic essay, *Citizen*. In an elegy for Trayvon Martin, the Black teenager fatally shot in 2012 by a neighborhood watch captain who found his appearance in their gated community "suspicious," Rankine writes: "Those years of and before me and my brothers, the years of passage, plantation, migration, of Jim Crow segregation, of poverty . . . accumulate into the hours inside our lives where we are all caught hanging, the rope inside us, the tree inside us, its roots our limbs" (89–90). These lines, like the works of Fanon and Coates, mark their allegiance to history by connecting present-day racial injustice with the collective memory of slavery. Rankine's image of the perpetual psychological lynching rope within "my brothers" implies that Black masculinity is permanently rooted to the historical brutalities of slavery and its subsequent violence. The legacy of the slave trade, that first horrific and involuntary journey, is indelible. How, then, can Americans move forward with the weight of that past history, and how can we move forward without it?

To answer this question, I turn to two contemporary African American women novelists, Toni Morrison and Jesmyn Ward, who depict the journeys of their male protagonists with both compassion and critique. As is the case with all the conversations in this book, the later author directly credits the influence of the former; Ward cites Morrison as one of her primary inspirations, describing her first experience reading *Beloved* as transformative: "Toni Morrison called me out of my wandering, her words, whole sentences, whole paragraphs, speaking to me as none had ever done so before" (*New York Times*). While *Sing, Unburied, Sing* most obviously parallels *Beloved* in its thematic interests in the roots of racism, the negotiation of trauma, and ghostly hauntings, it shares significant concerns with *Song of Solomon* in its use of a road trip to trace the personal development and evolving historical awareness of its male protagonist. Both Morrison and Ward use physical journeys to initiate historical journeys for their Black male protagonists who likewise seem to contain Rankine's images of the lethal rope and the more hopeful tree within them.

In both novels the road trip and its analogues represent attempted escapes from the ongoing bondage and baggage of racism, connecting metaphorically to the struggles of the characters' ancestors to escape the literal chains of slavery. The novels go on to imply that while ignorance of this troubled past motivates the men to flee, greater knowledge of their history leads to a more healing, sustaining connection with their community as a means to freedom. Morrison begins by depicting how her protagonist, Milkman Dead, feels stifled and irritated at home, where "everybody wants the life of a black man" (222). Over the course of his journey into the South, he comes to understand the nuances of that phrase and how it encompasses both the historical context of oppression and the benefits of an interdependent community of care. Ward uses the pilgrimage of young Jojo Stone to retrieve his incarcerated father as a way to explore poverty, drug addiction, and the prison industrial complex, depicting "the kind of world . . . that makes fools of the living and saints of them once they dead" (105). Jojo comes to learn that his Black body, just entering manhood, holds the power not only to threaten but to protect the community he calls his own. For both characters, the physical journey is requisite to initiating the historical one, demanding resolution of longstanding familial anguish. Part of this resolution involves the men's willingness to incorporate female narratives into their masculine ones, ultimately altering not only the male protagonists on their personal identity quests, but also the very homes and families they left behind. These two novels are just a few signposts on the lengthy literary journey that extends back to the haunted past, and gestures forward to a still-troubled future, so this chapter will make a few other literary stops along the way as well. Our embarkation point is Milkman's Michigan, in a luxury home he cannot wait to escape.

SONG OF SOLOMON'S HOME
(ONLY) AWAY FROM HOME

From the Middle Passage to the Green Book, from the Great Migration to fatal traffic stops, journeys for Black men in America have been fraught with danger, violence, and traumatic memory. Toni Morrison's Milkman Dead, however, is a character willfully ignorant of his own past and that of his country, and he embarks on a voyage South with little trepidation or fore-thought. He begins the novel as a reluctant resident of Michigan, a place that propels him to another place: "Once the people of the lake region discover [that they are landlocked], the longing to leave becomes acute, and a break from the area, therefore, is necessarily dream-bitten, but necessary nonethe-less" (*Song of Solomon* 162). The impetus for Milkman's journey away from Michigan is his not-home on Not Doctor Street near No Mercy Hospital, a series of negations that renders him rootless. Morrison's first lines often offer inversions of this kind; primers that miseducate, homes that fail to shelter, horses that rise like men.[2] Milkman's story, as Catherine Carr Lee observes, begins as an inversion of the hero's journey it seems to mirror: "Where the classic American initiation story takes the youthful initiate from the bosom of hearth and family, leaving him isolated and alone, Morrison begins with a twentieth-century modern man, alienated and fragmented, and ends with that man's successful connection with a people" (60). We see evidence of this "alienated and fragmented" state in Milkman's physical home. The well-appointed house of Ruth and Macon Dead appears ever more stifling, its complex familial dysfunction characterized by the heavy dining table's stub-bornly permanent water stain. That stain, like so much of Morrison's imagery, is an ineradicable reminder of the past: seeping from the daily flower vase demanded by Ruth's imperious father, it becomes a mark she weaponizes to remind her husband of her own superior birth, her elegance, her attunement to finer things. The house is the house of Milkman's grandfather, the patriarch both revered and feared, and the Dead family only ever exists in its shadow.

One space that belongs to Milkman's father without the burden of past history is his automobile; yet even this proves confining. This prototypical postwar American image of escape fails the Deads; Milkman's sister reflects that their family car, "Macon Dead's hearse," was always, like its daugh-ters, a mere showpiece to be used and abused: "us and the car, the car and us . . . first he displayed us, then he splayed us" (215–16). This contrasts, for example, the joyous journey Violet and Joe take to New York in Morrison's later novel, *Jazz*, when the train, the couple, and the city ahead all begin to move as one: "the trembling became the dancing under their feet . . . and like a million others, chests pounding, tracks controlling their feet, they stared out the windows for the first sight of the City that danced with them" (30, 32). In *Jazz,* travel is a euphoric possibility, and even the name of the railroad conveying the characters, Southern Sky, connotes flight. Milkman's view from the car window conveys the opposite imagery: Looking ahead, "he could see only the winged woman careening off the nose of the car," and looking backward is "like flying blind, and not knowing where he was going—just where he had been" (32). The statuette with wings, affixed to the hood, is a reminder of the flightlessness that so aggrieves him; looking backward feels like "flying blind" because Milkman has yet to understand the value of confronting "where he has been." These descriptions also foreshadow that a car will help bear Milkman back to the past, providing him the recognition of his own history prerequisite to future flight.

Milkman's comfortable life affords him an extended delay of the necessary confrontation with the historical trauma of his ancestors. Most of Morrison's characters, notably, do not have this luxury, and her other novels depict a much more direct confrontation with trauma. In *Beloved,* Morrison coins the term "rememory" to suggest the inadvertent recollections of trauma so powerful they can even manifest to others (43). The intensity of traumatic memories appears even in language, when the novel's protagonist, the former enslaved woman Sethe, feels "resigned to her rebellious brain. Why was there nothing it refused? No misery, no regret, no hateful picture too rotten to accept?" (83). Even as she tries to avoid picturing her horrific past, she uses the prefix "re" four times in these lines, linguistically revealing her repetition compulsion. In contrast, Milkman becomes irritated by any attempts of his parents to reveal their painful pasts, willfully perpetuating his own ignorance by believing that "he himself was not involved or in any way threatened" by the tribulations of his ancestors (74). In his introduction to *Black Skin, White Masks*, Frantz Fanon makes the radical argument, "I propose nothing short of the liberation of the man of color from himself" (8). Milkman is, in fact, in need of liberation from himself; in contrast to Sethe and other Morrison characters who have suffered intense trauma (such as Pecola Breedlove, Frank Money, and Bride), Milkman is the only one stunting his own growth, as symbolized by his psychogenic limp and bland acceptance of his infantilizing nickname. The novel suggests that only by understanding both history and its impact on the present can we stop limping along and start to liberate ourselves from ourselves.

Frantz Fanon, in his mid-century optimism, advocated skipping this step. At the end of *Black Skin, White Masks*, he argues for looking forward, claiming that in order to unburden ourselves from the weight of history both White and Black people "must turn their backs on the inhuman voices which were those of their respective ancestors in order that authentic communication be possible" (231). While this strategy certainly appealed to a younger Milkman, it eventually falls short upon his realization that he must attend closely to these "inhuman voices" of his predecessors, not dismiss them. As Morrison states in her essay "Rootedness: The Ancestor as Foundation," we must heed those from the past, because "when you kill the ancestor, you kill yourself" (344). Morrison warns against relinquishing familial heritage through a novel in which father loss weighs heavily, as it did on her at the time: Macon, Pilate, Ruth, Freddie, and Guitar, along with the author herself, have all lost their fathers. Reba and Hagar never know their fathers, and while this absence seems minimized in their merry malelessness, Hagar's love-starved self-annihilation betrays her longing for a paternal figure. Morrison confirms this in her "Rootedness" essay, stating that the generational line from Pilate to Reba to Hagar shows "a diminishing of their abilities because of the absence of men in a nourishing way in their lives" (344). Although the father of the Dead household still lives (if marginally), the ghost of Milkman's grandfather haunts it; both fail to provide support or solace. The tension between Ruth's excessive filial devotion and her husband's disgust over its necrophiliac oedipal connotations, both epitomized by and as intractable as the water stain on their table, fragments the couple and leaves the next generation isolated and rootless. Written in a more activist era, *Song of Solomon* urges its readers to reject such attempts to achieve racial harmony by turning away from the sins of the past.

MODELS OF MASCULINITY: SEEKING VALUE(S)

Milkman's journey out of Michigan progresses from North to South, reversing the path of the Great Migration that carried many, including Morrison's own parents, northward. As Catherine Carr Lee observes, Milkman's discovery one day that the people on the street are "all going the direction he was coming from" (qtd. in Lee 45) foreshadows how he "will have to move against the tide of black migration north" (Lee 45–46). This connection is even more apt in context: Everyone else on the street is processing the horrific murder of Emmett Till, an adolescent Northerner lynched in the South for allegedly whistling at a White woman. Milkman, indifferent to racial history, glibly foregrounds his own inconvenience over the boy's death: "Fuck Till. I'm the one in trouble" (*Song of Solomon* 88). The novel itself, otherwise meticulous about chronology, misdates Till's death in 1955 to 1953, as though Milkman privileges his personal narrative over historical fact enough to maneuver the event out of real time and into its appropriate place in his fictional one. Till's journey likewise parallels Milkman's as a Black Northerner in a Confederate state, which should act as a cosmic warning; yet Milkman so quickly forgets Till's murder that in Shalimar, Virginia he "wondered why black people ever left the South. Where he went, there wasn't a white face around, and the Negroes were as pleasant, wide-spirited, and self-contained as could be" (260). If the White faces (and white hoods) aren't visible, they don't exist to Milkman, who remains convinced that his status can insulate him from violence. Milkman's journey must undo this willful ignorance of both the history of slavery and the present of Jim Crow, for, as Lee points out, "this feeling of being at home (in the South) is still an extension of his sense of entitlement" (54). James Baldwin writes in his 1960 essay, "Fifth Avenue, Uptown," about an equally ignorant yet opposite question posed to him by "a very well-known American intellectual": "Why don't all the Negroes in the South move North?" (68). Sidestepping the naive implication that everyone has the income and ability to uproot and relocate at will, Baldwin explains that when Southerners move North, "They do not escape Jim Crow: they merely encounter another, not-less-deadly variety" (68). Unimpacted by either form of racism, Milkman maintains a sense of apathy towards racial injustices. His male role models do not share this luxury, however, and Milkman's journey is both driven by and reactive against their problematic responses to Jim Crow.

Milkman's indifference finds its foil in his friend Guitar's violent retribution. Adolescent Milkman learns to be a man predominantly by attaching to and mimicking Guitar Bains, until Guitar reveals his membership in a group dedicated to killing one innocent White person for every murdered innocent Black one. Their eventual falling-out over Guitar's political extremism parallels the real-life one of James Baldwin and Richard Wright: Both begin with the younger, Northern-born man idolizing the elder, Southern-born radical one, but eventually end in disillusionment. Shortly after Wright's death in 1960, Baldwin's complicated reflection on his legacy in the essay "Alas, Poor Richard" parallels how Milkman views Guitar: "The violence is gratuitous and compulsive because the root of the violence is never examined. The root is rage" (188). This parallel suggests what we might learn by connecting past to present, and by reading widely; men like Milkman and Guitar could benefit from considering that their conflict had precedent amongst Black intellectuals. Lacking Baldwin's perspective and insight about what motivates his friend, Milkman dismisses Guitar's legitimate grievances in favor of a mild passivity—"I live and let live"—which only converts into a more complex emotional register during his journey South (214). His subsequent understanding of history allows him to understand Guitar's motivations, if not necessarily his eye-for-an-eye methods. Although Milkman leaves his friend behind in favor of a solo quest, Guitar is everywhere; he is never far from Milkman's thoughts, and soon reappears on his trail. The racial injustices, past and present, that motivate Guitar's violence thus prove inescapable.

While Milkman chooses flight and Guitar chooses to fight, Macon Dead opts for ownership. Voraciously accumulating wealth without purpose,

he seems unaware of a past when some enslaved people, such as Halle in
Beloved, did so to purchase freedom. Understanding this history might give
him insight into the origins of his compulsive acquisition; as James Baldwin
empathically reflects in watching the eyes of an old Black Southerner: "he
had never in his life owned anything, not his wife, not his house, not his child,
which could not, at any instant, be taken from him by the power of white
people" ("Nobody Knows My Name" 110). As unaware of these inequities
as Guitar is obsessed with them, Milkman's other primary male role model
imparts to his son the primacy of possessing both homes and their residents:
"Let me tell you right now the one important thing you'll ever need to know:
Own things. And let the thing you own own other things. Then you'll own
yourself and other people too" (55).[3] Idolizing possessions to compensate for
losses both historical and personal, Macon elides the existence of slavery and
the fact that his own father was an owned object. His very name, an accidental
and inebriated coinage courtesy of the Freedman's Bureau, evinces this era-
sure; rather than change the mistaken moniker in a way that might bring him
Fanon's "liberation from himself," Macon Dead the First keeps it because,
"Mama liked it. Liked the name. Said it was new and would wipe out the
past" (54).[4] It does the reverse, of course, entrapping Macon and his name-
sake descendants in the same White man's joke, detaching them from their
own past and chaining them instead to the one chosen for them. Macon the
First ensnares his heir through his decision to ignore the past, both through
their shared name and his imposed concept of ownership, leaving his son a
false legacy that burdens rather than uplifting him.

THE PLANTATION LIVES ON

Milkman's journey South reveals that the familial obsession with owning
property is another way that the plantation era continues to keep them in
chains. Macon the First's willingness to die rather than relinquish his own
land leaves his children orphaned, yet his bereaved son draws the same mis-
taken conclusion that every plantation owner implicitly did: Property is worth
more than life. As Valerie Sweeney Prince puts it in her analysis of home in
the African American novel, the lesson young Macon receives is that "home
is untenable, yet it must be defended even at the cost of life itself" (122). In
sacrificing his life for his home, the first Macon Dead leaves his children
homeless, forcing them to hide in the mansion of the Butlers, the very people
who shot their father. Macon and his sister Pilate are trapped in a tiny hid-
den room while the family's Weimaraner dogs run free; their situation, and
the German name of the dogs, may allude to Anne Frank's excruciating
entrapment and imply solidarity between disparate historical instances of

oppression. The plantation home precedes the concentration camp, and it continues to enslave long after both were dismantled.

As the novel demonstrates, the plantation functions psychologically in part by perpetuating an insidious myth of "home." The Butler mansion later shifts from historical to mythical, revealing a witchy Circe, whose name and beasts connote Homer's *Odyssey* and whose ginger-scented abode suggests *Hansel and Gretel*. Morrison observes in her essay *Unspeakable Things Unspoken* that this is part of her "own giggle (in Afro-American terms) of the proto-myth of the journey to manhood," because "whenever characters are cloaked in Western fable, they are in deep trouble" (192). Farah Jasmine Griffin expands on this idea, noting that Morrison's allusion "questions the Homeric Quest, with all its plunder, traffic in women, slavery, and its seeking a return to re-establish the order of the patriarchy" (84). Milkman's story parallels Western mythology in its problematizing of what constitutes a home, and at what cost. Hansel and Gretel discover a tasty façade does not a safe haven make; Odysseus tarries with Circe for a year while neglecting the weaving wife who keeps his home fires burning. Morrison's Circe overvalues her overfurnished home, deciding that the best revenge on her former employers is to destroy the domicile they so cherished. Dedicating her existence to ensuring the Butlers' beloved dogs destroy their beloved mansion is a particularly futile form of posthumous revenge, leaving her living in excrement and decay long after her employers have died. By devoting her life—slavishly, one might say—to the destruction of a house instead of its upkeep as she once did, she is still valorizing the central importance of a plantation-style home over her own freedom.

Only Milkman's aunt Pilate, whose journeys inspire his own, seems to offer a viable alternative to plantation ideology. Her divergence from his father stems from their childhood: Macon's quarrel with Pilate over whether or not to keep the gold of a man they believe they killed divides the young siblings forever as each doubles down on their stance about value versus values; material gain versus spiritual solvency. Forsaking the gold, Pilate spends her youth unburdened with possessions and traversing the nation "as if her geography book had marked her to roam the country, planting her feet in each pink, yellow, blue, and green state" (148). As Laura Dubek observes, "her interest in geography reminds the reader not just of the segregated nature of American life in the mid-twentieth century, but also of the distance some black folks had traveled from their past" (94). Although Milkman fails to appreciate it at the time, Pilate is an inspiration for him to travel away from his physical home and back into his family history. Although Pilate is unbound to anyone or anything except that which she chooses, she willingly pursues peregrinations that continue to tie her to family and history, beginning in Virginia where she heard their "people" were and leading to Michigan to reunite with her unwelcoming brother. Milkman attempts to follow his father's avarice to the gold, but inadvertently trails Pilate's heritage back to the past.

Milkman's journey to the past leads him to the memories of his grandfather as they survive in the townspeople of Danville, revealing the origins of the opposing values embodied by his two children. Morrison moves the narration into the minds of the townspeople, recounting Macon the First as an inspiration to them all:

> We got a home in this rock, don't you see! Nobody starving in my home; nobody crying in my home, and if I got a home you got one too! Grab it. Grab this land! Take it, hold it, my brothers, make it, my brothers, shake it, squeeze it, turn it, twist it, beat it, kick it, kiss it, whip it, stomp it, dig it, plow it, seed it, reap it, rent it, buy it, sell it, own it, build it, multiply it, and pass it on—can you hear me? Pass it on! (235)

This passage moves interestingly from hospitality to rapacity. The first two lines could be spoken by Pilate, who willingly gives anything she has to others, and who opens her home to Milkman from the moment they meet. The remainder, however, offer a philosophy easily recognizable as Macon's, in which the land becomes something to abuse and destroy for personal gain. While the exploits of Milkman's grandfather live in legends, his grandmother's only legacy is that of her alleged Native American ancestry: a hint at an alternative perspective on land ownership, but one that Milkman must travel further in space and time to uncover.

Milkman's rude awakening upon arriving in a Confederate state highlights his ignorance of history and the still-extant racial and economic inequities apparent to the reader. Casually peacocking his wealth about to Virginian men with nothing to lose, he soon realizes that his Gatsby-style carelessness projects his father's condescending materialism: "He was telling them that they weren't men, that they relied on women and children for their food. And that the lint and tobacco in their pants pockets where dollar bills should have been was the measure. That thin shoes and suits with vests and smooth smooth hands were the measure" (266). The Southerners, still living with the daily deprivations and degradations of Jim Crow, respond by redefining masculinity on their own terms. They begin with a violent assault upon the newcomer followed by a ritualistic shaming via hunting expedition, in both cases shifting the terms of competition into physical rather than economic ones. Yet the Shalimar men's status at the bottom of the trash heap of life[5] is evident first in their sad scuffle over schoolboy taunts in a decrepit convenience store, and second in the fact that they hunt "coon," a pejorative term used to degrade Black hunters like themselves into the prey they seek.

The demeaning hunting expedition leads to an epiphanic moment for Milkman, as he begins shedding possessions in a physical unburdening and gradual unlearning of Macon's materialism. Intending to return laden with gold, he instead becomes progressively unencumbered: "all he had started out with on his journey was now gone" (277). Losses beyond the material infuse the hunting scene; first Milkman loses his breath, and then notices that as the darkness diminishes visibility, "the rest of him had disappeared" (277). Moments later he loses his only friend, as Guitar attempts to murder him; then he loses his posturing pride, confessing that he was "scared to death" (282); and, finally, he loses his characteristic limp, which was always "mostly in his mind" (62). The rupture and later loss of his last possession, his watch, suggests a necessary disruption of Milkman's single-minded focus on the here and now, and a movement away from a patriarchal fixation on time. Having shed so much, Milkman, whose self-perception is founded on a belief in his own exceptionalism, finally adopts Guitar's advice: that, like the peacock, if you "wanna fly, you got to give up the shit that weighs you down" (179). What weighs him down, in part, is the internalized plantation mentality inherited from his father that he must relinquish in order to fly free.

FLIGHT AND ROOTS

Both Milkman's lifelong hunger for flight, and his eventual realization that his great grandfather could literally fly, suggest the lingering fantasy of escape as a method of undoing the trauma of slavery. In a continuation of Morrison's inverted migration narrative and in keeping with the popular movement of the 1970s, Solomon flies out of Virginia and "back to Africa" (328). As James Baldwin describes, this movement offered a positive connection to history; whereas his own childhood was filled with negative connotations of Blackness, when "one was always being mercilessly scrubbed and polished, as though in the hope that a stain could thus be washed away," ("East River, Downtown" 80) by the early 1960s Black Americans had come to understand that "they were not merely the descendants of slaves in a white, Protestant, and puritan country: they were also related to kings and princes in an ancestral homeland, far away" (81). Ta-Nehisi Coates remembers his interest in the "back to Africa" movement around the same time: "Perhaps we should go back . . . Perhaps we should return to ourselves, to our own primordial streets, to our own ruggedness, to our own rude hair. Perhaps we should return to Mecca" (39). The movement began to lose favor with the advent of aviation and subsequent connections to colonialism, as Katherine Thorsteinson describes: "Greater contact with Africa has followed from this technological development, revealing important cultural differences

that make cross-Atlantic return a less ethically tenable solution . . . although
the myth originally expressed the desire to fly back to an Africa untouched
by slavery, this tradition could not have developed if Africans had not been
enslaved in the first place" (277). Despite this newer awareness of the colo-
nialist potential of Black Americans returning to Africa, however, the tradi-
tion continues for some. Olga Davis describes how contemporary pilgrimages
back to Africa can be both personally healing and "redefine the rhetorical
situation of slavery" (158). Milkman's discovery, at the height of this move-
ment, that his great-grandfather flew back across the ocean thus connects him
to an important facet of history and a way of transforming the past.

While Morrison's magical realist technique allows us to imagine the pos-
sibility of human flight, the fact that such an escape is only possible in the
pages of a novel leads the reader to consider the implications of such a fan-
tasy. As the ghost of his son, Jake, bemoans, "You can't just fly off and leave
a body," for the father purchased this superhuman power of flight at the price
of abandoning his wife and twenty-one children (209). Flightless Jake goes
on to marry his Native American adopted sister, thus keeping things in the
family and wedding his roots to those of his homeland. Morrison explains that
flight "is a part of black life, a positive, majestic thing, but there is a price to
pay—and the price is the children. The fathers may soar, they may triumph,
they may leave, but the children know who they are; they remember, half
in glory and half in accusation" (qtd in Krumholz 206).[6] Solomon's name
is immortalized in a fabled precipice, but his forsaken wife is the unhappy
namesake of "Ryna's Gulch": an absence, a lack, without even the poetry of
"valley" or "ravine" to its name.

Just as Pilate's family-centered definition of home contrasts Macon's
version of ownership and possession, so too does Pilate's commitment to
her people and history contrast the impossible dream of Solomon's flight.
Arguably the most unequivocally positive character penned by this author
who revels in moral ambiguity, Pilate consistently and instinctively honors
her heritage. Unlike Milkman, Pilate sensed the value of her history even
before she knew its details; as Susan Neal Mayberry riffs, Pilate "sings Sing's
sad song but carries Mr. Solomon's funny bones" (111), holding on to both
a tune and a corpse without recognizing their connection to her own life.
Appropriately, then, Milkman chooses to share his newfound knowledge first
with Pilate, instinctive keeper of their heritage; but in a debasing revision of
the traditional hero's homecoming, he triumphantly bursts into Pilate's home
only to receive a whack in the head and imprisonment in her cellar. In fact,
this recompense for his lethal callousness towards Hagar[7] and eventual recon-
ciliation with Pilate appears to be the only function of his short-lived home-
coming. Milkman revisits Michigan for a scant three pages before returning
to Shalimar; and, in contrast to Part I, which takes us from Milkman's birth

to his dubious manhood at age thirty-two, all of the travelogue in Part II occurs within about a month.[8] This timeline emphasizes journey over return; in contrast, *The Odyssey*, the hero's journey urtext, spends nearly half of its twenty-four chapters on the homecoming. Milkman, unlike Odysseus, finds that the women have not remained patiently awaiting the man's return; Hagar has received the unfortunate release of death, but Corinthians liberates herself in her brother's absence and finds her own employment and romance. Milkman's return home, therefore, leads him to genuine remorse that "while he dreamt of flying, Hagar was dying," (332) which in turn allows him to travel back to his family's homeland along with a now-reconciled Pilate: "peace circled her" (334).

Pilate's own life ends as soon as she and Milkman have buried her father, as though she could only rest upon doing so. As Susan Neal Mayberry puts it, however, navel-lacking Pilate "never truly dies just as she is never really born" (111). This is consonant with the book's frequent blurring of the lines between life and death: Solomon's "leap" to freedom mirrors a suicidal one; Ruth and Pilate share a "close and supportive posthumous communication with their fathers" (*Song of Solomon* 139); and of course, Milkman's whole family is walking around "already Dead" (89). Each of these instances reminds the reader that this past is not finished, and that we must take these stories with us into the present day. Pilate falls down beside her father, requests one last song, and dies as her name flies away with a bird; she thus closes the loop of her family history by leaving her body with her father on the earth while her spirit moves towards her mother Sing in the sky. In this moment, Milkman sees that Pilate accomplished what Solomon couldn't: "without ever leaving the ground, she could fly" (336). Pilate's story lives on, demonstrating that only in understanding the stories of family, community, and history can we truly take flight.

Song of Solomon began as an exercise in empathy: Toni Morrison cites the origin of as the recent death of her beloved father and desire to understand what the men he knew were "really like" (xii). She sees her novel as enacting "a radical shift in imagination from a female locus to a male one," but the centrality of Pilate's role complicates this idea (xii). I would contend that the book presents less of a "radical shift" from Morrison's gynocentric works and more of a motion towards interdependence and community. Although Milkman plans a solo venture, the trip he takes becomes collaborative, intergenerational, and simultaneously masculine (spatial, airborne) and feminine (temporal, narratological). The novel suggests that pilgrimages require both connection and balance. As Morrison later explained of her beloved character, Pilate is "the best of that which is female and the best of that which is male" ("Rootedness" 344). Milkman should learn from his aunt and, as his name implies, reconcile the feminine "milk" with the "man." Flight and roots, present and history, masculine and feminine, change both the home Milkman left behind and the journey he pursues. Its tragic conclusion, however, suggests that these balances are aspirational ones of an imagined future, rather than realities achieved within the text and the time.

Milkman's journey lacks closure, ending not with Pilate's transcendence but with Guitar's vengeance. The intensity and competition between the men simmers towards hostility at many points; as James Baldwin writes of his aforementioned relationship with Richard Wright, "who has not hated his black brother? Simply *because* he is black, *because* he is brother. And who has not dreamed of violence?" ("Alas, Poor Richard" 213). This sentiment directly parallels Guitar's visions of retribution for hate crimes (his "mind was on the wonders of TNT" [181]), while also suggesting that emotional closeness can, in fact, be a catalyst for aggression. The intensity of the relationship between Guitar and Milkman amplifies and calcifies their differences; although Milkman has undergone some significant transformation towards a more communal human outlook, Guitar retains his previous perception of him as pampered and self-centered. Perhaps if the two men had journeyed together from the beginning, they might have reached a point of reconciliation and been able to work mutually towards social change.

Reading *Song of Solomon* through a lens of radical empathy allows a contemporary reader to fit together the pieces of Milkman's story in a way he is never able to do. The legacy of slavery causes the characters to fight for freedom using the same means their ancestors did: escape, violence, and owning whatever they could. Neither flight, which risks abandoning those left behind, nor violence and ownership, which recreate the methods of the slave-owners, appear as sufficient responses. Instead, Morrison proposes Pilate's example: learning from the past, passing those stories on, and healing from collective trauma through community.

This interpretation helps clarify the ambiguity of Milkman's final leap onto Guitar and the novel's refusal to tell us "which one of them would give up his ghost in the killing arms of his brother" (337). Morrison later offers a positive view of their (possible) murder/suicide, referring to Milkman's final leap as "the marriage of surrender and domination, acceptance and rule, commitment to a group *through* ultimate isolation" ("Unspeakable Things Unspoken" 191). Catherine Carr Lee similarly interprets the ending as a "triumphant hope of continuation for an interconnected African American culture and heritage" (60). These optimistic perspectives look ahead, offering hope for their readers that, notably, is not available to the characters themselves. The deaths at the end indicate a problem of timing: Guitar spots Milkman at just the wrong moment; Pilate rises at precisely the wrong time to intercept the bullet intended for Milkman. This climactic and catastrophic lack of synchronicity, specifically in the context of a novel preoccupied with history, suggests that the timing is not yet right for liberation; Guitar's claim that "everybody wants a black man's life" gains emphasis when repeated in Milkman's last words (281). Milkman travels to the past, as Laura Dubek discusses, deepening his understanding of his "people" in both the local and larger sense, including "the many thousands gone, all the Africans lost during the Middle Passage and all the slaves who worked the land and suffered the lash" (99–100). This is a beginning but one that remains open-ended rather than foreclosed or resolved. The novel ends, perhaps not coincidentally, just before the Civil Rights Act of 1964. Milkman's final movement is towards that future, and the novel asks readers to help create a world where we all can fly without leaving our roots in the ground.

SING, UNBURIED, SING:
HEADING OUT, LOOKING BACK

Forty years later, Jesmyn Ward's *Sing, Unburied, Sing* takes another Black male on a Southern journey into his grandfather's past. Ward's loss of her brother is at the crux of all her writings; like Morrison's father loss, it may have inspired her to empathically inhabit the internal workings of male characters, notably in *Where the Line Bleeds* and *Sing, Unburied, Sing*. Reading Ward's novel as an answer to Morrison's illuminates the ongoing need for Black men to escape the confines of racism past and present, and similarly calls readers to consider the community we can create in response both within and outside of fiction. Although Ward's protagonist, Jojo Stone, similarly begins a voyage instigated by his broken home, his journey to Parchman prison for his father's release will take him through and beyond the past that Milkman cannot escape.

Jojo, like Milkman, suffers from parental neglect, but one compounded by harsh poverty rather than careless privilege. While Morrison gives us a psychological understanding of her protagonist's difficult parents, Ward offers a sociological one: Michael and Leonie are victims of, as Greg Chase puts it, "the criminalization of poverty—an institutional problem that has disproportionally affected communities of color" (210). Ward envisions these ills inscribed on male bodies literally and indelibly. Michael tattoos Jojo's name and baby feet on his back, indicative of how he will forever turn his back on his son, even leaving his inked incarnation to the mercy of the other dangers inscribed there as well: a dragon, scythe, and grim reaper. Leonie perceives her own father's tattoos, two cranes representing her and her brother Given, not as "a sign of life," but as one more indicator of injustice: her brother's crane is "poised in flight" while hers is "beak down in the mud" (*Sing, Unburied, Sing* 212). This perception recalls Morrison's depiction of how the men taking flight often leave the women behind; except here, and in Ward's own life, the brothers abandon their sisters unintentionally, through death. Beleaguered by resentment, grief, and addiction, Leonie can neither provide a home for her son nor find comfort in the one she and Given were given.

While Morrison's novel spans Milkman's entire life, Ward's centers on Jojo at age thirteen, negotiating his nascent manhood. As mature for his age as Milkman is stunted for his, Jojo compensates for his absent father by emulating his grandfather, River Stone, whom he calls "Pop" and who lives up to the moniker as a strong paternal presence. Jojo opens the novel with his belief that the ability to stomach River's slaughter of a goat for his thirteenth birthday dinner is what Morrison calls the "measure" of his manhood. Over the course of his journey, however, he reevaluates this standard of masculinity. Jojo viscerally rejects the goat slaughter because he empathically senses the animal's pain; the reader thus sees from the beginning that his manhood, like River's, is stronger because it contains the culturally feminized power of experiencing and enduring the pain of others. This empathic ability extends backwards through the maternal line, as River describes: "The dream of [my mother] was the glow of a spent fire on a cold night: warm and welcoming. It was the only way I could untether my spirit from myself, let it fly high as a kite in them fields" (23). These lines couple the ideas of flight and home that Milkman desperately attempts to reconcile, and they depict a solid maternal presence unlike that available to any of the three Macon Deads. Ward models empathy through these compassionate males; River is a man because of his mother, and Jojo must become a man in spite of his, fortified by his grandmother's legacy.

While Milkman leaves his home unemotionally and without apparent regret, Jojo departs on his journey by embracing River, who tells him "You a man, you hear?" but also says with his "pleading eyes" and "without words: I love you, boy. I love you" (61). In addition to offering a version of masculinity tempered by care, this moment is, according to Eden Wales Freedman, emblematic of the dual-witnessing that the two enact for each other, and that Jojo is able to perform for other characters later in the novel: "he does not cling too long to Pop or override his grandfather's narrative with tales of his own. He embraces the primary witness, then releases him" (170). Though firmly tied to home and family, Jojo, too, must leave it to recover the narrative of his grandfather's trauma because, as his grandmother explains, "Your pop don't know how to tell a story straight" (67). As is the case for Milkman, this is not a story that *can* be told straight; River will always "leave out something important in the middle" because he can't find a way to articulate his guilt and pain to his grandson or even to himself (67). Fiction is sometimes the only way to encounter such untellable stories, and even the reader must receive

River's story in fragments, perhaps leaving time to process each horror before we hear more.

This form of storytelling alludes back to Faulkner, whose influence on both Morrison and Ward is profound. Morrison wrote her master's thesis on his works, and notes "in a very personal way as a reader, William Faulkner had an enormous effect on me, an enormous effect" (Taylor-Guthrie 25).[9] Ward, who shares with Faulkner the conflicted legacy of a Mississippi childhood, states, "Faulkner is a huge influence, I really admire his work" (217). With this in mind, *Sing, Unburied, Sing* can be read not only as a response to *Song of Solomon* but also as an homage to Faulkner's *As I Lay Dying*, sharing with it the form of chapters that shift perspective, as well as the topic of a morbid dysfunctional family road trip in which the destination is only an unfulfilled promise of forward movement. Faulkner's description of his characters' journey applies equally to Ward's: "We go on, with a motion so soporific, so dreamlike as to be uninferant of progress, as though time and not space were decreasing between us and it" (107–8). Ward revises the inertia of Faulkner's plodding, mule-drawn wagon into the drug "trips" of its characters, which similarly promise progress but result in stagnation; her impoverished Black characters are as stuck in twenty-first-century Bois Sauvage as Faulkner's poor White ones were in twentieth-century Yoknapatawpha County. As Greg Chase observes, "Ward's own work becomes a means not just of supplementing Faulkner's legacy but also of correcting its racial blind spots, offering a kind of redress to the rural Southern communities about which they both have written" (201). Ward gives us the voices and thoughts of Mississippians impacted by poverty, as Faulkner does, but she also reveals a systemic racism visible in every possible form of incarceration.

PRISONS WITHIN AND WITHOUT

Before Jojo and his family arrive at the physical prison, they stop at two meth houses offering users the promise of escape while simultaneously ensnaring them in addiction. The two homes are a study in class contrast, showing the differences between wealthy and impoverished drug dealers, but they also parallel each other as though to emphasize the impossibility of evading their lure: both are seductive traps, deterring Jojo's real journey; both are filled with substances yet lack substance; Al's "cooking spoon" recalls the meth "cooking" in the lower-class house; both reference dreams of tropical isles while subverting any dreams of elsewhere; and although Al speaks in elegant lawyer language, we still see his incipient decay in his rotting teeth. Most tellingly, Al lovingly refers to his urn full of meth as "my Baby: my Beloved," which serves both as a nod to Morrison's novel and to the chilling fact that, to many of the characters, drugs are more beloved than their babies (148). As in Faulkner, the journey often seems impossible to complete, and as in Morrison, the drug houses promise "flight" but only at the cost of destroying families left behind. These false promises of escape only tempt the travelers into prisons both metaphorical and literal.

The car itself proves another false promise of escape. Ward, like Morrison, inverts the expected road trip narrative; as Nicole Dib points out, the car "traditionally symbolizes the promise of freedom expressed as free movement for all" (134), yet here creates claustrophobic confinement. Anna Hartnell expands on this in summarizing a 2013 interview with Jesmyn Ward, explaining that cars can become an obstacle to freedom as well as a facilitator of it: "the 'freedom' that cars have offered to Americans has, since World War II, led to urban sprawl, the atomization of communities, and the devastation of the environment" (205). In this novel, the vehicle is a mobile prison, and the destination is a literal prison; everyone is in chains, either actual or metaphorical. Catherine Calloway discusses the ways each of the main characters is imprisoned, often by sociological factors, all of which connect in some way to the image of the prison itself. Parchman Penitentiary, she argues, "illustrates well the liminal existence of the characters, who are caught between different worlds and are denied the spaces that would extend to them opportunities for social renewal or personal growth" (57). While prisons can have this purgatorial aspect of suspension and waiting, or even the more positive connotations of "reformatories," Parchman appears here as more of a full-stop than a place of liminal potential, destroying adults and children, prisoners and prostitutes, innocent and guilty alike.

Parchman achieves this effect by being built on the site of a former plantation and continuing to enforce terror through constant surveillance. A panopticon with no opportunity for privacy, where prisoners are forced to act as guards, becomes, as River describes, "the kind of place that fool you into thinking it ain't no prison . . . because ain't no walls" (21). In a novel where the characters struggle to progress, Parchman represents a past made ever-present. In fact, in *Worse Than Slavery*, a source Ward consulted for her novel, historian David Oshinsky describes Parchman as "the quintessential penal farm, the closest thing to slavery that survived the Civil War" (2). Parchman in Ward's depiction continues its legacy as a site of enslavement by rendering mercy and punishment equally random: River was jailed for housing his brother ("harboring a fugitive") and then freed for murder ("capturing a fugitive"). As Greg Chase notes, "such passages emphasize how Parchman—even more than most Jim Crow–era prisons—replicated the conditions of chattel slavery as they existed in the antebellum South" (211). Plantation and prison alike become the only home its victims ever know. The ghost of the slain twelve-year-old Richie reflects: "I wonder if the reason

I couldn't leave Parchman before Jojo came was because it was a sort of home to me: terrible and formative as the iron leash that chains dogs" (*Sing, Unburied, Sing* 190–91). Like Claudia Rankine's "rope inside," Parchman internalizes enslavement, creating a seemingly unbreakable chain of inter-generational trauma.

Rankine further articulates this internalized prison in a video script called "In Memory of Trayvon Martin," writing, "My brothers are notorious. They have not been to prison. They have been imprisoned. The prison is not a place you enter. It is no place" (*Citizen* 89). The gender-specific word "brothers" is indicative of the fact that Black men are at far greater risk of incarceration than women of any race; 93.2% of the prison population is male, according to the Federal Bureau of Prison. Ward knows well how close any young Black man always is to imprisonment or worse at the hands of police; as she writes in her memoir, *Men We Reaped*, "Trouble for the black men of my family meant police. It was easier and harder to be male; men were given more freedom but threatened with less freedom" (99). This threat of "less freedom" shapes Jojo's whole life, growing up as he does with a father in prison. When a policeman stops the family car and holds Jojo, an unarmed Black teenager, at gunpoint, and Jojo reaches towards his pocket, the conclusion seems inevitable to a contemporary reader. But Jojo, seeking the comfort of the *gris gris* bag his grandfather gave him for protection, receives the protection of another loved one, Kayla, who vomits on the officer. Though Jojo escapes, the encounter leaves scars, as he bears the lingering sensation that "the cuffs cut all the way down to the bone" (172). He comes to learn what Richie did; claiming he is more world-wearied than Jojo at thirteen, Richie explains that he already "knew that metal shackles could grow into the skin" (185). Like William Blake's "mind-forg'd manacles," these shackles become internalized until they can never be removed (poetryfoundation.org). When later eyed by a store clerk, Jojo recalls that his physicality announces itself as a threat: "I remember I'm brown, and I move back" (175). The cuffs, long removed, continue to cut.

While Jojo's encounter with the police is brief and not fatal, the novel bears witness to those whose handcuffs were never removed by alluding to the many Black men killed in police custody. The dying plea of both Eric Gardner and George Floyd, "I can't breathe," appears repeatedly, along with myriad references to troubled breathing and suffocation (65, 97, 126, 128, 274). Leonie loses her beloved brother to gunfire, rather than vehicular homicide as the author did; the fact that Given is gunned down by a White man who is rapidly exculpated for the crime gives his death a resonance with that of Trayvon Martin. Some of the ghosts haunting the family home at the conclusion even wear hoodies like Trayvon's, and one of them protests, as so many Black men have, "I put my hands up and he shot me eight times" (282).

Racial violence shifts, but never disappears; as Richie says of Parchman, "it's like a snake that sheds its skin. The outside look different when the scales change, but the inside always the same" (172). Just as Parchman embodies slavery in another form, police violence seems an updated Parchman. No journey can provide Jojo a true escape from that reality.

MAN OF THE HOUSE

Jojo successfully survives his many tribulations; despite hunger, thirst, neglect, and his brush with the law, he returns home. Like Milkman, however, he finds that home is not the same in the end, as it has been irrevocably altered by the death of a woman he loves. Following his journey, however, Jojo is able to reassess his family bonds and affirm his grandparents as parents. Michael's surname is erased by remaining unstated, as Jojo chooses to be a Stone, honoring his grandparents. In musing that Richie "could be made of stone," Jojo verbally inducts the lost boy's ghost into his found family as well.[10] The book concludes with Jojo trying to "be a man" once again with River, this time by feigning stoicism over his grandmother's death; eventually, however, he succumbs to tears, a movement towards a different kind of manhood (223). Jojo's true rite of passage is his ability to request and absorb River's horrific prison story, acting as a rock for River while understanding that the Stones are not made of stone: "I hold Pop like I hold Kayla" (257). A protector like River and a visionary like his grandmother, both loving and strong, Jojo, like Pilate, creates a home out of community. Significantly, he completes his pilgrimage after his journey has ended, returning home before releasing Richie's ghost from Parchman and releasing River from the haunting memory of it. In this way, as Nicole Dib writes, "The mold of the return home as a moment of identity creation for a single traveler is broken and replaced with a multivocal meeting" (149). *Song of Solomon*'s Pilate aspires to just this sort of "multivocal meaning," but Milkman fails to realize its potential. For Jojo, the iconic car provides no escape, but as the returned traveler he learns more about his community than about himself.

In contrast, Leonie is unable to surmount her grief to provide sustenance, nurture, or a home for her family. Jojo describes his mother as a "water moccasin," a snake also known as a cottonmouth, which could be a literal representation of the effects of chronic meth use on Leonie (209). In *Song of Solomon,* Macon recounts an essentialist fable to Milkman in which a snake bites the very man who saved it and reared it, claiming its nature as excuse: "you knew I was a snake, didn't you?" (55). Jojo views Leonie like this fabled snake, incapable of doing anything but poisoning those she loves. Reflecting on her fatal neglect of his pet fish, Jojo realizes his mother "ain't never healed nothing or grown nothing in her life . . . Leonie kill things" (*Sing, Unburied, Sing* 107–8). His grandmother is the only character able to use Leonie's lethality for good, enlisting her daughter to assist her in dying: "Like I drew the veil back so you could walk in this life, you'll help me draw it back so I can walk in the next" (216). Aiding her mother's release from cancer is one thing Leonie can do properly and selflessly, turning her destructive nature to good use. This generosity is short-lived, however, and she soon escapes for her own pilgrimage with Michael, abandoning their children to return to the road. Ward reflected in an interview that cars "become these places where we're able to be introspective and reflect and connect in certain ways"—ways so profound, in fact, that "it makes me think of the ways that church can function, or has functioned in the past, in the community" (Hartnell 214). For Leonie, the car becomes a debased version of this church metaphor where she communes only with herself and Michael. As Leonie reflects, "the car shrinks the world to this: me and him in this dome of glass" (*Sing, Unburied, Sing* 274), which recalls Jojo's image of his starved pet fish while also describing the endless drug trip they pursue alone in their self-created bell jar.

Jojo and Kayla, however, manage to stitch the scraps of nurturing Leonie provided into something whole. In the final transformation of home, the children exorcise the ghosts using the best they have gleaned from their inconsistent mother. While Jojo releases both River and Richie from the mental imprisonment of Parchman, Richie seems purgatorially stuck between here and hereafter. He cannot enter the Stone home again because "there has to be some need, some lack," and Jojo no longer suffers from these; nor can he enter the afterlife and "Become. The song" until Kayla intervenes (281). Throughout the road trip Jojo rubs Kayla's back in circles of eternal comfort; in the conclusion, Kayla disperses the ghosts with a similar circular movement, and Jojo grudgingly remembers, "it's how Leonie rubbed my back, rubbed Kayla's back" (284). Kayla sings, like Pilate does, a song from her origins: "like she remembers the sound of the water in Leonie's womb . . . she sings it" (285).[11] In song, in movement, the children use the little mothering they have received to comfort the ghosts of the traumatized. Compassion and care complete Jojo's journey to manhood, reminding the reader of the way we all can help combat the legacies of a traumatic past.

The ghosts who haunt the house may be placated, but they never depart the yard. They remain roosting in a tree, which, as Eden Wales Freedman discusses, simultaneously connotes Jesus' fatal cross, the lynching trees, and the Stone family tree, aptly evoking how this considerable historical trauma is rooted in their own backyard. The persistence of the ghosts can seem foreboding. Kirsten Dillender writes that the novel cautions us to "treat grand narratives of racial progress pessimistically, suggesting that instead, black subjects

must acknowledge the impact of the past on the present before they can pre-
pare for futures unfettered by structural antiblackness" (132). Dillender views
the final scene as indicative 'of the paltry historical progress achieved from
slavery to the present day: "Ward's ghosts underscore the truth that in the end,
there is little substantial difference between the deaths of Given and Richie
and the enslaved blacks who came before them" (135). I read Ward's conclu-
sion more psychologically, demonstrative of the hope afforded by reconciling
past and present. The ghosts do not depart, as trauma never does, but they are
part of a communal voice. Richie's journey all along has been an attempt to
understand his own death, not necessarily overcome it: "The place is the song
and I'm going to be part of the song" (183). By hearing River's story both
with and through Jojo, Richie is released to join the other ghosts: not at rest,
but no longer alone. As Kayla sings and circles, they act collectively: "they
smile with something like relief, something like remembrance, something
like ease. *Yes*" (284). These lines, especially the final Joycean affirmation,
suggest a closure for both children and ghosts. The Stone children are still
parentless, still poor, still facing a future stacked against them. However,
they also possess both compassion and second sight; they can nurture both
humans and spirits. Though the ghosts do not depart yet—and perhaps some
never will—the novel concludes with their final direction, the journey's end:
"Home" (285).

CONCLUSION: SHARED STORIES AND SONGS

Reading Jesmyn Ward in conversation with Toni Morrison, and connect-
ing both to Black male writers such as Fanon, Baldwin, Coates, and oth-
ers, reveals that the journey into the past that Milkman and Jojo undergo is
imperative for not only these characters but their authors and readers as well.
In *Black Skin, White Masks*, Fanon describes racism as a kind of "collective
catharsis" (144) and calls attention to the longstanding use of Black men to
represent "the Wolf, the Devil, the Evil Spirit, the Bad Man, the Savage"
(146). He discusses his own realization of this phenomenon: "I was respon-
sible at the same time for my body, for my race, for my ancestors" (112).
Both Morrison and Ward respond to these ingrained stereotypes of Black men
and attempt to write their way out of them. The two male protagonists create
an interesting contrast; while sociological factors weigh on them both, the
impact of poverty and neglect is far more apparent for Jojo, a boy who must
grow up too quickly, than for Milkman, a man remaining a child too long. Yet
both must reconcile their family heritage and the historical impacts of slavery
before moving into manhood.

In both novels, written by women but focusing on men, a balanced view of gender is requisite for the protagonist's journey. According to Rolland Murray, only in Milkman's "recuperation of his own family history does one see the rupture of the patriarchal paradigms that drive most of the novel's male elites. Milkman's quest for self-discovery leads him beyond purely patriarchal preoccupations to complicated dual-gendered historical narratives" (130). Milkman's disdain for women is consistent and characterological: He finds his mother "too insubstantial, too shadowy for love"; dismisses Hagar as no more than "the third beer . . . the one you drink because it's there"; and urinates on his sisters both literally and figuratively, as Lena reminds him: "all your life . . . using us, ordering us, and judging us" (75, 91, 215). Only on his journey back to the past does Milkman recognize Pilate's importance in his life and narrative and come to accept assistance and knowledge from other women, such as Circe, Sweet, and Susan Byrd. If he is not capable of fully transcending his patriarchal inheritance, he is on the path of understanding how to do so.

Jojo's youth is his strength in negotiating gender paradigms; as he is still struggling to become a man, he is open to learning from and caring for women. By the novel's conclusion he claims both grandparents as his family legacy, and even Leonie can see that he is "hard as Pop and soft as Mama" (271). Having witnessed the death of his grandmother and the release of the ghost of his uncle, Jojo has matured: "all the little boy gone from his eyes" (272). Yet he still requires his baby sister Kayla to help him bring the ghosts peace at the end. As Nicole Dib writes, the novel's conclusion "does put hope in kinship, however fragmented or damaged, that can emerge even between the living and the dead" (149). Brother and sister, past and present, people and ghosts, all come into balance in this ending, and that balance provides a glimmer of hope in a very dark coming-of-age tale. Jojo's future is still in the process of becoming.

Milkman does not return home at the end of the novel; his pilgrimage, though transformative, ends in loss and death. Furthermore, the fact that the Black men in the book can only fly at the price of abandoning those they love implies that freedom remained unattainable for a Black man in the 1960s and 1970s. In a call-and-response that echoes the Biblical "Song of Songs" alluded to in the novel's title, Hagar and Ruth argue over the unrequited "anaconda love" they both hold for Milkman: "He is my home in the world" "And I am his" (137). Milkman never finds a true home of his own in a physical location or in any woman's arms. Instead, Morrison's novel demonstrates the complexity of the obstacles, societal and psychological, confronting Black men in their journey to fulfillment, leaving the reader in some doubt as to whether they can be successfully surmounted. Laura Dubek observes that this uncertainty can be seen from the very origin point of the novel's story, including that Milkman's grandfather moved to what would become Not-Doctor Street the very year that *Plessy v. Ferguson* made "separate but equal" the law of the land: "By framing the novel's opening scene—Robert Smith's suicidal leap off the roof of Mercy hospital in 1931 Detroit—with local history and geography, Morrison begins with the assertion that the promise of freedom for black Americans has gone unfulfilled" (93). It seems that by the time of her writing the novel over forty years later, that promise of freedom remained an empty one.

Jojo, in contrast, returns home and comes to terms with the merciful brutality of his grandfather's past, releasing the ghosts that have been haunting the Stones. Embodying a new kind of masculinity, Jojo seems poised to break the familial cycle of incarceration. As Ward said in an interview with Anna Hartnell, "I do think it's important in fiction to end with hope. Hope equals meaning, and for me there has to be some sense of meaning to any story, to whatever I write" (216). That hope rests in Jojo's ability to create a community through his family. When Richie suggests that Jojo has yet to learn about love, Jojo mutely points to Kayla, not even requiring words to demonstrate his devotion to his sister. He has always had his "home in the world" with a beloved female family member, in contrast to Milkman. Neither protagonist would be able to complete their journeys without the help of loved ones, nor without the ability to learn from and emulate their generosity and compassion. While this lesson comes too late for Milkman, Jojo seems poised to learn from his journey into the past. Read together, then, the pilgrimages of these two Black men illuminate not only the distances we have traveled historically but also the progress yet to be made.

Finally, these novels ask their readers to continue on the journeys they have begun. Nicole Dib reminds us that Ward's novel "does not release us from the 'something to be done' that racial haunting puts into the world" (149). Rabbi Tarfon, as paraphrased by Annie Dillard, describes this aptly: "This work is not yours to finish, but neither are you free to take no part in it" (202). In other words, we must find a way to participate in the ongoing struggle against racism that these books define, even if that struggle is bound to continue long after us as well. Eden Wales Freedman describes how both authors (influenced by Faulkner, as described above) offer us a sense of the importance of witnessing authentically:

> Instead of asking readers to witness what they sense they cannot (as Faulkner does), Morrison and Ward accomplish what their readers may have not (yet): they testify (through fiction) to the multiethnic, nonpatriarchal, enslaved, and traumatic experiences at the heart of American personhood, literature, and history and then invite us to take up their mantle and carry their work forward into the real world. (179)

This may seem much to ask of one's audience. But both authors show how, for their protagonists, the journey is worth what sometimes seems a nearly incomprehensible level of challenge and sacrifice. Physical movement grants emotional insight, and only by looking backward can we imagine how to move forward. Morrison and Ward, two Black women writers, imagine themselves in the place of Black men; these Black men, in turn, learn to appreciate and understand the Black women in their lives. As readers, we learn to look beyond our own subject positions and gain empathic understanding not only from and of our own ancestors but also from and of those we find in the pages of novels.

NOTES

1. Coates cites the origin of his title as a Richard Wright poem, adding to the legacy list of Black writers.

2. See the openings of *The Bluest Eye*, *Beloved*, and *Home*, respectively.

3. Railroad Tommy offers a disquisition to Milkman and Guitar about all they, as Black men, will never have, including a wide array of comforts, accolades, and luxury goods (60). His list has a Lacanian focus on the way that lack shapes the lives of Black men; how the not-having becomes their self-definition. Milkman, however, suffers more from excess than from deprivation.

4. Guitar, in contrast, owns his slave name and makes it his own: "Guitar is *my* name. Bains is the slave master's name. And I'm *all* of that. Slave name doesn't bother me, but slave status does" (160).

5. This image appears in Morrison's first novel, *The Bluest Eye*, when Cholly's mother abandons him on a literal trash heap, and society abandons his daughter on a metaphorical one: "all of our waste which we dumped on her and which she absorbed" (205).

6. Morrison expands on this, writing in "Unspeakable Things Unspoken" that although Western mythology can prove heavily problematic, "the African myth is also contaminated" (192). Robert Stepto responds in *A Home Elsewhere*, observing how, in texts like *Song of Solomon*, a story becomes "a 'contaminated' myth if its real and abiding work is to 'mythologize desertion'" (70).

7. See Michael Awkward's essay, which "foregrounds not only Milkman's archeological question, but also Hagar's disintegration" (89).

8. Milkman leaves in September of 1963 and returns in early fall.

9. Immediately afterwards she seemed to regret the statement and claimed, implausibly, that Faulkner had no effect on her writing.

10. Richie has always seen himself as a Stone, saying of River, "Him my big brother. Him, my father" (135).

11. The call and response that Pilate and Reba sing at Hagar's funeral also has interesting parallels to this scene.

Chapter Four

Trees in Concrete

Shifting Classes and Changing Neighborhoods in Sandra Cisneros and Kali Fajardo-Anstine

Is home the place where you feel safe? What about those whose home isn't safe? Are they homeless, or is home an ideal just out of reach, like heaven? Is home something you move toward instead of going back? Homesickness, then, would be a malaise not for a place left behind, but one remembered in the future.

—Sandra Cisneros, "Chocolate and Donuts"

SANDRA CISNEROS: A QUESTION OF CLASS (AND GENDER AND RACE)

According to Cherríe Moraga, editor of the foundational collection *This Bridge Called My Back*, "the dirtiest five-letter word in 'America' is 'C-L-A-S-S'" ("Catching Fire" xviii). She explains how class inequalities necessarily intersect with liberation movements for women of color, concluding by passing the torch through writing to her readers, calling out to "those young people who may pick up this collection of poems, protests, and prayers and suddenly, without warning, feel their own consciousnesses catch fire" (xxiv). In the previous chapter, we explored how African American authors proposed supportive gender-inclusive communities as a means of counteracting the lingering escapist and violent responses to the aftermath of slavery. The Chicana authors in this chapter suggest a place for these communities through storytelling, narrative, and writing, highlighting how readers can

75

participate in the process and take action in their own communities. Both writers imply that such writing and reading are crucial to creating a space where everyone can feel at home, a concept they depict as both threatened and desired by the working poor.

This community begins, as we have seen, with authors inspiring other authors. In a 1991 interview with NPR, Sandra Cisneros discussed the success of her young adult novella *The House on Mango Street* and expressed her hope that other Latine[1] authors would enjoy similar acclaim: "I think I can't be happy if I'm the only one that's getting published by Random House when I know there are such magnificent writers—both Latinos and Latinas, both Chicanos and Chicanas—in the U.S. whose books are not published by mainstream presses or whom the mainstream isn't even aware of" (qtd. in Ganz 27).[2] Cisneros implies here that she cannot even celebrate her own success so long as she celebrates it alone, suggesting that one of the critical functions of art to her is that it spurs others to create more art. She also specifically addresses Chicanas, her own self-identification, which succinctly expresses her Mexican heritage, gender, and class; when asked what makes someone a Chicana beyond a "Spanish surname," she replied, "someone who has the political consciousness, and that means the class consciousness to write about things that haven't been written about because they're issues that mainstream society doesn't necessarily want to hear. They're writing about struggles and working class people and oppression and pain" (qtd. in Torres 223). Kali Fajardo-Anstine is but one of many younger Chicana authors inspired and encouraged by Cisneros, crediting her in an interview as "an enormous influence" (Luna). Cisneros's endorsement appears on the cover of Fajado-Anstine's first short story collection, *Sabrina and Corina*, proclaiming: "These stories blaze like wildfire." In turn, Fajardo-Anstine writes in the Acknowledgements section of *Woman of Light*: "To Sandra Cisneros, whose work showed me how to dream" (308). Their work shares particular connections around the importance of neighborhood dynamics, gentrification, and class mobility, all part of a literary conversation that began with a single house on Mango Street.

Throughout *The House on Mango Street*, the young narrator, Esperanza Cordero, articulates her desire for an eventual house of her own—a desire so strong that one critic notes, "this emotion drives the narrative sequence and character development in the entire collection" (Mujcinovic 107). The chapter about her house precedes even the one about her name, and the desire for "a real house. One I could point to" (5) is perhaps the primary hope implied by the translation of "Esperanza." The final chapter, in contrast, reflects back on the house that was never a home: the "sad red house, the house I belong but do not belong to" (110). Fueling Esperanza's hope, a fortune-teller, Elenita, promises that she will one day achieve "a house made of heart" (64).

Esperanza's disappointing house, her fantasized dream house, and her neighborhood community all shape her intersectional identity intertwining gender, race, and class.

Esperanza's first friend on Mango Street informs her that they will only be friends for a week, because "the neighborhood is getting bad," by which she means Brown (13). Therefore, Esperanza sagely reflects, Cathy and her family will "have to move a little father north from Mango Street, a little farther away each time people like us keep moving in" (13). Cathy's brief appearance in the book and in Esperanza's life is consumed by fear of her neighbors; she cautions against speaking to various residents on the grounds that they are "full of danger," "raggedy as rats," "smell like a broom" (12, 14), all implicitly racially inflected critiques in context. The one person she does not consider beneath her, Alicia, is the one she suspects might be above her: "stuck up ever since she went to college" (12). In this comment she attempts to put the aspirational Alicia back in her "place," and simultaneously caution Esperanza against any such notions of self-improvement.

In her final appearance, Cathy defends the house her father built, claiming that the steps, which Esperanza describes as "all lopsided and jutting like crooked teeth," were "made that way on purpose" to help the "rain slide off" (22). Cathy's redefining of her house's flaws defensively avoids identification and connection with her neighbors and their own imperfect DIY home improvement projects, reinforcing her belief in her White family's superiority. After Cathy's family departs in a clear example of "white flight," the Spanish-speaking Ortiz family moves in, and subsequently rents the basement to a Puerto Rican family. The house that Cathy's father built now belongs to those she was taught to fear. With their departure, Mango Street becomes, at least through Esperanza's descriptions, almost entirely segregated; the people in her world are predominantly of Mexican heritage and near-exclusively Latines.

This segregation is cyclical: racism leads to segregated neighborhoods, which lead to further racism. As Fatima Mujcinovic observes, *Mango Street*'s "depiction of class and ethnic hierarchies emphasizes the idea of social segregation: although legally prohibited, the division of social space and life is still perpetuated by ever-present racial/class inequalities" (107). White flight and its subsequent racial segregation were well-known to Cisneros in her own Chicago community and have been the subject of concern since the 1950s and into the present day. Linda Zou, a psychology professor at the University of Maryland, found that the motivating fear has not dissipated but rather shifted from centering around Black people to "foreign" people, including Latines: "The more that white Americans perceived this foreign cultural threat, the more they reported wanting to move out of those communities" ("White Flight"). Even those who claim to be open to integrated neighborhoods don't necessarily choose to live in one. And increasing diversity has sometimes led to greater prejudice rather than acceptance; Latines make up over half the total population growth in the United States, and as Zou observes, "those changing racial demographics may trigger heightened perceptions of threat among white Americans and contribute to the persistence of segregation" ("White Flight"). With this segregation comes increased financial disparities, larger educational gaps, and myriad subsequent social ills.

Mango Street suggests that, for reasons both cultural and economic, this segregation enforces the cycle of poverty, increasingly entrapping "the ones who cannot out" (110). Seeking models of the woman she wants to become, Esperanza's adolescent perspective focuses on the plight of the neighborhood women, many of whom are locked inside their houses. Her grandmother and Rafaela gaze longingly out their windows; her friend Sally, only a few years older than Esperanza herself, is barred from even that small mercy. Lilijana Burcar critiques the novel on Marxist grounds, disputing this privileging of gender over class: "Poverty is not problematized as constructs of gender are in this novel. Instead, it is merely alluded to in descriptive and static terms and presented as yet another among many of the unrelated phenomena that plague the narrator in her childhood and late teenage-hood" (31). She specifically opposes interpretations influenced by intersectionality, which, she claims, "flattens and thus redefines class as one with gender and race, that is, as merely another in a series of oppressions" (29). Lisa Orr, though more open to intersectional readings, also notes that class is underrepresented in fiction of the *Mango Street* era: "It is as if the writers of the 1980s could take for granted a certain sophistication about race that was absent when it came to class" (86). To listen to the novella on its own terms, however, rather than wishing it to conform to a particular political agenda, is to be open to "embracing a paradigm of race, class, and gender as interlocking systems of oppression," as Patricia Hill Collins advocates (222). Mango Street itself is an embodiment of these "interlocking systems of oppression," as it is Latine, and poor, and particularly oppressive to women, and each of these elements influences and interacts with the others. Attempting to understand this dynamic as uniquely created by all these factors may offer a greater level of "sophistication," as Orr advocates.

Esperanza's account of her first job offers one example for this kind of intersectional reading. The chapter begins defensively, uncertainly: "It wasn't as if I didn't want to work," she tells us, observing that her family needs money because "The Catholic school cost a lot, and Papa said no one went to public school unless you wanted to turn out bad" (53). As is the case throughout Cisneros's work, these deceptively simple phrases contain multiple implications: the opening "wasn't as if I didn't want," contrasted by the reference to the cost of school, demonstrates that labor is financially necessary, even for a young girl who must lie about her age to gain it. The choice of Catholic school (with its value implicit in its high cost), immediately followed by the judgmental "turn out bad," is culturally determined.[3] Elsewhere Esperanza infers that she will probably "go to hell" and "deserve to be there," demonstrating her deep internalization of Catholic distinctions between good and evil (58). Finally, Esperanza's first day on her first job concludes in her first sexual assault via an older coworker's unwelcome kiss. Being Mexican brings her to Mango Street which has, allegedly, poor public schools; being Catholic necessitates a high-priced school and thus a job while underage; being female and underage/naïve ends in sexual assault. Earl Shorris evocatively terms this "the surround of force," referring to the legion of obstacles obstructing the path of those like Esperanza and, to an even greater degree, "the ones who cannot leave as easily" as she can (105).

Cisneros explicitly uses *Mango Street* to demonstrate this "surround of force" in all its complexity. In an interview she stated that the novella was "a reaction against those people who want to make our *barrios* look like Sesame Street," because "poor neighborhoods lose their charm after dark. . . . I was writing about it in the most real sense that I know, as a person walking those neighborhoods with a vagina" (Rodriguez-Aranda 69). This reflection explicitly connects race, gender, and class as intersectional factors in Cisneros's own life, and as conscious components of her writing. In her essay "Notes to a Young(er) Writer," she reflects on the economic advantages that Emily Dickinson had, including education, a house, and a maid, which potentially countered some of the obstacles she experienced as a woman. This spurs her to muse about the untold stories of those lacking such privileges: "I wonder if Emily Dickinson's Irish housekeeper wrote poetry or if she ever had the secret desire to study and be anything besides a housekeeper" (75). In her subsequent short story collection, *Woman Hollering Creek*, Cisneros features several protagonists whose class is a greater obstacle than their gender. For example, in "Eleven" a thoughtless teacher ruins Rachel's birthday by foisting a raggedy and unattractive sweater upon her, insisting it is hers and publicly shaming her in the process. In "Barbie-Q" two young girls can only afford their beloved plastic dolls when the toy warehouse burns down and discounts the drenched, soot-coated, and slightly melted remnants. Even in these examples, gender and class intertwine. We might consider the beauty standards implicit in clothing for a girl on the cusp of puberty, or the impossible body image projected by the famously unrealistic Barbie dolls, respectively. While gender takes the leading role in many of *Mango Street*'s anecdotes, the economic challenges of its protagonist consistently compound these struggles in a way they could not have for Dickinson.

THE IMPACT OF COMMUNITY

The influence of community on the individual is widely known and heavily
theorized, notably in the branch of philosophy known as communitarianism.
In *Liberalism and the Limits of Justice*, Michael Sandel claims that "com-
munitarianism is not optional: we cannot conceptualize the individual apart
from his or her community, its practices, culture and values. The commu-
nity constitutes the person" (qtd. in Frazer and Lacey 108). It would seem
impossible to separate Esperanza from her community, particularly because
it is relatively static: while the White neighbors may flee, most of the resi-
dents remain in place due to both cultural affinity and lack of opportunities
to move elsewhere. Michelle Tokarczyk's study of working-class female
authors, including Cisneros, led her to observe that in both these works and
her own experience working-class neighborhoods may have an even stron-
ger than average emphasis on community: "because working-class people
must labor together and aid one another when in need, their culture values
solidarity and group identification rather than individual achievement" and
that "working-class people are often closer to their ethnic origins" (23).
Although she adds the caveat that "working-class culture is actually a vari-
ety of cultures" (23), totalizing neighborhoods in this way remains a broad
generalization; nevertheless, it does seem to apply to the denizens of Mango
Street. Just as Esperanza's selfhood is comprised and formed by her intersec-
tional positions, so too is her community, which shapes her in turn. Macarena
García-Avello writes of these interdependencies: "Cisneros's stress on the
community rather than the individual suggests that the self is necessarily
dependent on others. Thus, Mango Street, along with the people and stories
that inhabit it, cannot be separated from the construction of Esperanza's sub-
jectivity" (73). The construction of the book itself, in which we learn much
about Esperanza through her stories of the community around her, confirms
this idea. So do the community members themselves, in fact; the three sisters
(*comadres*) of the novel bring Esperanza this message: "You will always
be Mango street" (105); and college-educated Alicia repeats it: "Like it or
not you are Mango street" (107). She is and always will be the place of her
upbringing; the individual is inseparable from the community.

This interdependency, while unavoidable, may or may not be undesirable.
Alicia's phrase "like it or not" indicates a certain level of ambivalence that
may derive from her broader perspective gained from college. Esperanza, the
author, and the reader may all share some conflicted feelings about what it
means to be ontologically inseparable from your place of origin. On the one
hand, that sense of community engenders joy, such as when Esperanza, her
sister, and their neighbors buy a bike together in what she describes as "Our

Good Day" (14). In making this purchase Esperanza willfully rejects Cathy's judgmentalism, knowing that her alliance with Lucy and Rachel may end their friendship—and indeed, this is their last interaction we witness before Cathy moves away. But the bike brings the girls delight, and so does their ongoing friendship, despite a few bumps in the road. Even when the neighbors bicker, the very inventiveness of their mud-slinging, including epithets like "chicken lips," "cockroach jelly," and "cold frijoles," seems to contribute to Esperanza's imagination and eventual literary ambitions (37). The community of Mango Street provides very fertile friendships.

While the other young girls of Mango Street energize and nurture Esperanza, the wider community often seems to hold her back. When the friends acquire a set of high-heeled shoes, they revel in their costumery until a drunk man offers them a dollar for a kiss, quickly shifting innocent dress-up into tawdry prostitution. Esperanza's liminal position between childhood and adulthood allows her to see across both boundaries. Together, the four girls—Esperanza, Nenny, Lucy, and Rachel—parallel the "Four Skinny Trees" that inspire Esperanza to such poetry in one of the book's most well-known chapters:

> Four who do not belong here but are here. . . . Their strength is secret. They send ferocious roots beneath the ground. They grow up and they grow down and grab the earth between their hairy toes and bite the sky with violent teeth and never quit their anger. This is how they keep.
>
> Let one forget his reason for being, they'd all droop like tulips in a glass, each with their arms around the other. Keep, keep, keep, trees say when I sleep. They teach. . . .
>
> Four who grew despite concrete. Four who reach and do not forget to reach. Four whose only reason is to be and be. (74–75)

This passage depicts the girls as the source of empowerment for one another, each member propping up the other three. Esperanza's neighbors (the trees) give her strength, even as the neighborhood itself (the concrete) holds them back with all its might. Cisneros parallels this imagery in speaking of her own upbringing in contrast to those of her peers at the prestigious Iowa Writer's Workshop: "My classmates were from the best schools in the country. They had been bred as fine hothouse flowers. I was a yellow weed among the city's cracks" (*Publishers Weekly*). These weeds, like the skinny trees, appear as tenacious survivors emerging out of their suffocating environment. The implicit contrast between people and their space, organic humanity and entrapping buildings, complicates the concept of "neighborhood," and deepens Esperanza's ambivalence about leaving and returning.

As discussed in Chapter Three, flight has its costs, and those who escape always leave behind those who cannot. Due to the story's limited focus on one brief period of time, we do not learn the fate of most of the residents of Mango Street, and even the lucky few who are able to escape the concrete constraints do so at some personal cost. Jason Frydman speaks to these challenges by noting that Esperanza's ambitions are not free of internal conflict: "Esperanza fears paralysis, fears not moving, fears not being upwardly mobile" (20). While the book is typically read as a positive depiction of upward mobility, detailing the path of escape for our young protagonist, Frydman problematizes that view through a Freudian-deconstructive consideration of the text's uncanniness and instability. He observes that "celebrating its reconciliation of individual development and community solidarity represses the cost and the fragility of that reconciliation, and thereby establishes another neurotic pattern" (22). If we are not attentive to the psychological cost of being one of the few trees to grow despite the concrete, we risk ignoring all the others trapped beneath its weight. *Mango Street* ends, significantly, with Esperanza's dream of escape "one day," but not with its actuality (110). Leaving her poised on the brink of adulthood, hopeful but uncertain, reminds the reader that even those feisty trees are rooted to Mango Street. As Michelle Tokarczyk writes, "Growing up as an American does not mean severing the roots of home, which is an especially important point for working-class people for whom upward mobility has seemingly required cultural amnesia" (65). If we imagine that the book itself is authored by an adult Esperanza, living in her own home but writing of the one she left, then we understand that she has indeed "gone away to come back" (*Mango Street* 110). It is a very rare person indeed who can leave without "severing the roots" and transplant themselves successfully.[4]

FROM WHITE FLIGHT TO GENTRIFICATION

When Esperanza fantasizes about leaving Mango Street, she pictures her community as static and fixed. Neighborhoods, however, tend to be subject to change, particularly through gentrification. First coined in 1965 by British sociologist Ruth Glass, "gentrification" refers to what happens when "all or most of the original working class occupiers are displaced and the whole social character of the district is changed" (qtd. in Sanneh). Reflecting back on one of her earlier childhood homes in the essay *"Tenemos* Layaway," Cisneros observes that old Chicago brownstones like the shabby one she resided in could have been restored to their former glory, but "we lived in neighborhoods destined for the urban expansion of the University of Illinois" (185). Esperanza, with her youthful and generous heart, hopes to resist this gentrification by blurring the distinction between her working-class self and the unhoused population:

> One day I'll own my own house, but I won't forget who I am or where I came from. Passing bums will ask, Can I come in? I'll offer them the attic, ask them to stay, because I know how it is to be without a house.
>
> Some days after dinner, guests and I will sit in front of a fire. Floorboards will squeak upstairs. The attic grumbling.
>
> Rats? they'll ask.
>
> Bums, I'll say, and I'll be happy. (86–87)

As a child she chooses to remember what so many of us choose to forget: how it felt when we most needed the help of others. In her fantasy she constructs a dream home where she retains her private space—the rest of the house—but reserves the separate attic for those in need. In reality, however, the lines dividing wealthy and impoverished, housed and unhoused, can prove more difficult to cross.

Institutionalized racial divides have a long history, from explicit redlining to subtler deterrents. When I was house-hunting in 2005, the realtor recommended looking West of Federal Boulevard because on the East side the "houses wouldn't have the same resale value"—meaning, I later discovered, that that was where the predominantly Mexican community lived. While the racism in this example is rather overt, even seemingly innocuous practices like the preservation of historic districts can have a similarly detrimental effect. June Dwyer examines the implicit racism and classism of historic districts and the laws protecting them, pointing to their reliance on a "historical record" that generally overlooks the rights or preservation of non-White cultural communities. Dwyer argues that, contrary to popular belief, "cultural self-assertion on the part of ethnic homeowners brings both innovation and vitality to their adopted neighborhoods" (166). She discusses Cisneros's renegade act of painting her house "Corsican purple," a shade which, despite its European name, remained off-limits in her historic district of the formerly Spanish, formerly Mexican, city of San Antonio, Texas: "In response to the demand that she conform to established standards, she defended her purple casita on the grounds that vernacular ethnic architecture has a historic role in articulating living spaces and, in so doing, made the case that ethnic populations have improved the environments in which they have settled" (165). In fact, this same case had apparently been made in the construction of the bold red San Antonio Central Library (by a Mexican architect) just a few years before. Why was the library lauded and the casita condemned? Perhaps one begot the other, gradually building a public resistance to excessive coloration, or rather to *demasiado* Chicano.

Historical preservation is thus a self-selecting and self-perpetuating process, one that decides which history is preserved, so that it can be further protected, and which can fade until forgotten. In her essay "My Purple House," Cisneros herself observed this paradox:

> My history is made up of a community whose homes were so poor and unimportant as to be considered unworthy of historic preservation. No famous architect designed the houses of the Tejanos, and there are no books in the San Antonio Conservation Society library about the houses of the working-class community, no photos romanticizing their poverty, no ladies auxiliary working toward preserving their presence. Their homes are gone, their history is invisible.

Historic preservation is intended to keep something—houses, history—visible. Ironically, the solution to the Great Purple Caper came through the diminished visibility wrought by the standard ravages of time: the house faded into what was deemed an "acceptable color." This provides an apt metaphor for its chillingly implicit lesson: People of color are welcome here, as long as they stay muted.

The real-life tumult over the purple house, like Esperanza's fictionalized experiences, is an intersection of class as well as race. Although the bright color hearkens back to Mexico, and to a Mexican American aesthetic that Cisneros describes as "more is more," it is also a way to elevate status and create beauty with little investment ("*Tenemos* Layaway" 186). Cisneros describes this in her essay "¡*Que Vivan Los Colores!*": "No one wants to live like they're poor, not even the poor. The poor prefer to live like kings. That's why they paint their houses with the only wealth they have—spirit" (174). She repeats this idea several times throughout her work, testifying to the importance of art, beauty, aesthetic pleasure—not in spite of urban blight but because of it.

After seventeen years, and with some regrets, Cisneros decided to part with her purple casita. Seeking to relocate to Mexico in her later years, Cisneros expressed dismay in "*Mi Casa es Su Casa*" that in purchasing any home she would necessarily be "displacing someone's *viejitos*" no matter which house she chose or how willingly sold it was (360). She ruefully concluded, "I am part of the gentrification" (360). This is, of course, unavoidable; as communitarianism instructs, even with the best intentions no individual can avoid all separate choices that have larger systemic effects on neighborhoods and communities. What Cisneros's book is able to do, however, is call our attention to the impacts such choices have on communities. When Cathy's family moves away, they are part of White flight; when Esperanza departs, she will contribute to brain drain. While any individual's decision to move is unlikely to be impacted by this awareness, we may at least hope to gain more insight into the dynamics of the communities we enter, and those we leave behind.

KALI FAJARDO-ANSTINE: INFLUENCES AND INTERSECTIONS

Cisneros observes that she and other Latina writers "are inspiring a whole younger generation of women, just by our mere existence, just by being, just by stepping in the classroom . . . it's a ripple effect that's going to help those eleven-year-olds out there reading *House on Mango Street* in a way that will save them from being lost in the desert" (Torres 218). Fajardo-Anstine may once have been one such eleven-year-old. In addition to openly acknowledging Cisneros's influence, Fajardo-Anstine shares much with her predecessor, including a Chicana/mixed heritage, a talent for writing in the voice of middle school girls, and a family of seven children.[5] Like Cisneros, she writes of the impact on community from her own working-class background: "we were not, as they say, well-to-do," as she puts it ("On the 32" 12:50). And, like Cisneros, she had to find a new way to incorporate these aspects of selfhood into her fiction, despite a literary world that often has little place for them. She, too, may inspire many who would otherwise be "lost in the desert."

Fajardo-Anstine gained much inspiration from reading, but, as she stated in her keynote address at Regis University in 2021, she lacked a space where she could read in peace, so "the bus became one of my classrooms" ("On the 32" 18:50). The reverse also seems true: that books become a means of transportation. Despite all books could offer, they did not entirely allow her to see herself reflected in the authors or characters; she aspired to be a writer but could not imagine entering that unfamiliar territory: "The reason I never dreamed it was possible . . . I never saw characters like me in literature" (20:05–20:19). Fajardo-Anstine tells of a particularly chilling conversation at West Side Books, where she worked. An older customer gestured towards the wealth of volumes surrounding them and remarked, "'Look around you . . . What possibly could you contribute that hasn't already been said?' 'A lot, I said—my people, for the most part—we aren't in any of these'" (18:05–18:20). Even without the explicit discouragement of strangers in your workplace, this feeling haunts many writers of color. The fictitious Azteca Intergalactic series, beloved of the titular character in "Tomi," may hint at this reality: The only Latines Tomi sees in literature appear in science fiction, in impossible situations on alien worlds. Like Afro-Futurism, this "Aztec Futurism" might be a way of reclaiming connections to an ancestry lost through enslavement and colonization, but the disconnect between fantasy and reality is palpable. Reading the stories together, Tomi and his aunt wonder, "where does blood spurt in zero gravity and are jaguar teeth and obsidian spikes still the preferred weapons?" (*Sabrina and Corina* 155). Their questions emphasize how little these futuristic Aztecs have in common with the daily lives of their earthbound counterparts. In contrast, the story "Tomi" itself is overtly realist, complete with the names of real places and a story that shows genuine human failing and connection. Fajardo-Anstine has written her way into the bookshelves that once excluded her.

Despite experiencing similar crises of confidence around breaking boundaries as a Latina writer, Cisneros notes that her background and its struggles helped forge her own unique voice. She had access to a different source of creativity than her more privileged peers in Iowa's prestigious creative writing program: "What did I know except third-floor flats. Surely my classmates knew nothing about that. That's precisely what I chose to write: about third-floor flats, and fear of rats, and drunk husbands sending rocks through windows, anything as far from the poetic as possible" ("Ghosts" 73). Yet Cisneros's writing, and Fajardo-Anstine's, is quite poetic—often when their subject matter is the least so, such as in their descriptions of domestic violence. In describing abused women of the neighborhood, Cisneros writes of how Minerva "is always sad like a house on fire" (*Mango Street* 84), and how Sally's father "forgot he was her father between the buckle and the belt" (93), and how Rafaela, locked in her home by her jealous husband, pines for sweet drinks to contrast a life that tastes "bitter like an empty room" (80). In the titular story of *Woman Hollering Creek*, Cisneros details how a man beats his wife "until the lip split and bled an orchid of blood" (47). Fajardo-Anstine eloquently describes Luz's mother in *Woman of Light* drowning in alcohol and her own sadness after being abandoned by her abusive husband: "Her eyes didn't focus—they glimmered black and wet, as if she lived in a realm without any sunrise, stuck inside the ether of her own design" (82). In "Cheesman Park," the narrator compares her own beaten face to "rotting fruit" and "some gruesome mask" (*Sabrina and Corina* 121, 132). As Corina applies her cosmetology skills to her murdered cousin Sabrina's corpse in the eponymous story, she reflects, "Her hair shone like spilled motor oil, greens and golds and blues in all that black. Corkscrewed sections bounced off my curling iron, more alive than anything on that table" (38). Corina, in fact, summarizes all of these narratives succinctly after her cousin's death, when she reflects on "how men loved her too much, how little she loved herself, how in the end it killed her. The stories always ended the same, only different girls died" (44). What is the cord that binds Cordovas and Corderos alike: nourishing umbilical, or lethal garrote? Or are the two linked, so that what ties these women to family and home ultimately strangles them? In their incongruously beautiful descriptions of brutality, both authors refuse to allow their readers the luxury of turning aside, or of making easy assumptions about these women and their gruesome fates.

An intimate partner has committed some form of physical violence to one in three women in the United States, and a severe form to one in four, according to the Fact Sheet for the National Coalition Against Domestic Violence (ncadv.org/statistics). Women of color and women living in poverty are at even higher risk. This is a familiar story for both of these authors. Fajardo-Anstine commented in an interview with Maria V. Luna, "I came out of a lot of violence in my childhood," and observed that she had to develop a "hardened shell" as a result. Both authors' beautiful descriptions, often voiced by young narrators, emphasize the way such pervasive violence is so often ignored. Simultaneously, they force their readers to examine more closely something that has become a mere statistic, banal and easily overlooked. The jarring discordance between graceful language and horrific subject matter renders the topic impossible to overlook; How can we not envision orchids of blood, or dead hair like motor oil? As readers, we slow our attention and focus on these sinister details in defiance of the natural repugnance that cautions us to look away. Both authors use their fiction to open doors to their own communities—perhaps as an act of defiance, and perhaps as an act of preservation.

SABRINA AND CORINA: GENTRIFICATION AND LOSS OF COMMUNITY

Fajardo-Anstine recollects the shame her younger self experienced in driving by her Denver home with a potential love interest: "I pointed out my old house—the porch where I had broken the window with an errant softball. The back steps where I had fallen and permanently scarred my face" ("On the 32" 16:20). Her embarrassment at seeing her derelict home through the eyes of an outsider parallels Esperanza's humiliation when a passing nun sees the house on Mango Street: "I had to look where she pointed—the paint peeling, wooden bars papa had nailed on the windows so we wouldn't fall out . . . it made me feel like nothing" (5). For both writers, class as defined by geography, space, neighborhood, and house ownership prove central means of self-definition.

Fajardo-Anstine's short story collection *Sabrina and Corina* focuses heavily on geography, particularly urban neighborhoods around Denver, and thus parallels Cisneros's emphasis on space as a determinant of identity. Gentrification appears in these stories as a means of seeing in real time how shifting demographics systematically exclude the working class and especially people of color. June Dwyer describes the changes in Cisneros's neighborhood of San Antonio: "The gentrification had raised property values and made the neighborhood more aesthetically pleasing. This was by no means a bad thing, but it highlighted the tendency of gentrification to erase the presence of the lower classes, especially those who are not white" (175). "Aesthetically pleasing" is, of course, subjective (notably excluding aforementioned purple casitas), and Fajardo-Anstine's view of gentrification is much more sinister. As she told to an interviewer at *Westword* shortly after the release of *Sabrina and Corina*:

> I think the book is a love song to Denver as I know it, a multicultural space, a convergence zone where the various cultures that made me came together in a unique blend. My ancestors migrated north from southern Colorado in the 1920s and 1930s. They came to Denver for a better life, for work, and for their dreams of owning property. Many of our family homes in Denver are gone now due to gentrification and the financial and psychic stresses it causes a displaced people.

Fajardo-Anstine's experience is an increasingly common one. According to a study by the National Community Reinvestment Coalition, Denver—both the author's home city and my own—is the second most intensely gentrifying city in the nation, surpassed only by San Francisco (Richardson et al). The increasingly overpriced Northside neighborhood where I live and work was, in my childhood, an immigrant Italian community; it is currently pushing its more recent Latine residents further and further outside the city borders, where they face either diminished work opportunities or lengthy commutes. *The Denver Post* notes that "The Northside, the northwest Denver community that includes the Highland neighborhood, has been hit particularly hard by gentrification, with Highland's Hispanic population decreasing from 37% of the community to 16% in the past decade, according to U.S. census data," and that we are now "a community with some of the highest levels of Hispanic displacement nationally from 2000 to 2010" (Hernandez, "Where We Come From"). Gentrification causes both racial segregation and a diminishment of the city's distinctive character, so that what Fajardo-Anstine so aptly describes as "a multicultural space, a convergence zone" is fading fast.

Not everyone regrets that transformation, however. Fajardo-Anstine cites an incredible comment from a local resident near Regis University: "The poor people have had their time here, but now they have to go further North from the city. It's just the way it is. Those of us with money—we can take care of the houses better" ("On the 32" 21:37–21:48). The speaker valorizes houses over people in this statement,[6] but Fajardo-Anstine refuses to take that bait, responding only to the central flawed premise: "One thing I know about the 'poor people' I grew up with: it's that they cared for their homes more than anything, because it's a miracle . . . that they were able to afford them in the first place" (21:55–22:15). Cisneros agrees, reminiscing in "*Tenemos Layaway*" on her childhood neighborhoods: "Even the poorest of houses, the most beat up and scruffy and *fregadas*, the ones families rent but don't own, are sometimes the ones with the most pride. A tin of flowers in a lard can. A window full of cheerful Halloween decorations. A ton of Christmas lights even if the screen door is hanging like a broken jaw. 'We may be poor, but you can bet we're proud'" (185). Fajardo-Anstine's "miracle" resonates poetically with Cisneros's "ton of Christmas lights," both conveying a sense of spiritual wonder at human resilience and tenacity while contradicting the easy assumption that scruffy houses imply negligent owners. Both authors interrogate what exactly it might mean to take "better" care of houses and ask that we seek a more complicated story in the coexistence of the broken screen door and the bright flowers.

Furthermore, gentrification is not the only sociological problem creating struggles for racial equity in neighborhoods. *New Yorker* journalist Kelefa Sanneh observes that the reversal of gentrification does not create a simple solution: "The opposite of gentrification is not a quirky and charming enclave that stays affordable forever; the opposite of gentrification is a decline in prices that reflects the transformation of a once desirable neighborhood into one that is looking more like a ghetto every day." In other words, shifts in the desirability of neighborhoods, either up or down, can lead to the same unfortunate outcome: economic and racial segregation. In Fajardo-Anstine's story "Galapago," we see hints of this ghettoization problem, as the elderly Pearla Ortiz struggles to find a way to relocate out of her increasingly dangerous environs. She reflects on the possibility of "saving money, taking in laundry or boarders, anything to afford a home in a better neighborhood. Maybe north towards the Italians on Lowell or east towards the Jews by the university" (*Sabrina and Corina* 116–7). In this assessment, the ethnic communities are clearly divided, and lives are at stake: Pearla is not murdered by the knife-wielding intruder she encounters, but she must kill him in self-defense, leading to life-long guilt and her own eventual displacement into assisted living. As Sanneh summarizes, "In the ghetto narrative, a poor neighborhood falls victim to isolation; in the gentrification narrative, a poor neighborhood falls victim to invasion." Both, he notes, impact populations unequally; both can have devastating impacts on their residents who remain.

Sabrina and Corina takes the reader from ghettoization to gentrification: In "All Her Names" we return to the same Galapago Street where Fajardo-Anstine herself once lived, at a later time. The home of Alicia's *abuela* is now being sold by "an Anglo woman in a purple dress gingerly directing a group of exterminators," a statement implicitly connecting the former tenants to more "vermin" to be removed by the new ones (186). The ghetto that one generation could not afford to leave becomes the desirable neighborhood their progeny cannot afford to keep. In a time before indigenous land acknowledgements became *de rigueur*, Alicia reflects on how Confluence Park (its name again connoting the "convergence zone" Fajardo-Anstine embraces) was once an Arapahoe camp, but "now it was a desolate hillside filled with stoners and the homeless, flanked by multimillion-dollar condos and public art. The new Queen City of the Plains" (185). She responds with a passion for graffiti, illegal street art aimed to counter the expensive public displays she derides. Her partner in crime, however, mocks her complicity with the moniker "my little gentrification Malinche," alluding to the Aztec woman who betrayed her people to Cortés and the Spanish colonizers. Malinche, like Alicia, bore many names, and both women lash out as a result of their private pain: Malinche had been abused and enslaved by the people she sold out, while Alicia's "inability to spend an evening alone" and consequent infidelities likely stem from her parent loss (180). And, like Malinche, Alicia is a complex character, marrying into a neighborhood where she "walked alongside their designer strollers on Saturday mornings," (183) yet still choosing to risk jailtime over her graffiti pastime, because "someone has to make these invasive yuppies uncomfortable"—even if it's one of their own (181).[7] This internal conflict between her current yuppie life and her past heritage demonstrably leads to self-hatred in Alicia, suggesting another reason she is unwilling to spend evenings alone. Michelle Tokarczyk notes that while Malinche has been seen as "the source of self-hatred among some Mexicans and Mexican-Americans because the genesis of the *mestiza* people was in violation and betrayal," the character can be and has been rewritten (103). In fact, she concludes, "many Chicana feminists," including Cisneros, "are challenging gender stereotypes and restrictions by revising the role of La Malinche" (103). Alicia is one such revision, as she refuses to follow Malinche's path in birthing mixed-race children, seeking out herbal abortifacients from her Abuela Lopez rather than bearing her White husband's child. Unlike Malinche, who birthed Cortés's child, the protagonist of "All Her Names" will never possess one particular name: "Mother." If Alicia is connected to an Aztec heritage all the way back to Malinche, she will not pass it on, and her *abuela*'s legacy lies in her memories and her cures, not in the neighborhood, home, or another generation to inherit it.

While "All Her Names" concludes with Alicia appearing lost in her vacation home, unable to locate even the North star, "Tomi" traces the trajectory of Cole finding her way back home in multiple senses. After serving several years of prison time, Cole discovers that her neighborhood has altered dramatically during her involuntary absence: "The gentrification reminded me of tornados, demolishing one block while casually leaving another intact" (142). Amidst this image of destruction lies the stalwart presence of Cole's childhood home, now owned by her brother. When Cole remarks on a shiny new glass high-rise building that has displaced a nearby abandoned warehouse, her brother replies, "Yeah, real fancy. It also ruins my view of the stadium. Those property taxes are fucking me . . . but we were here first. I'll be damned before I move to the suburbs" (142–43). This tenacity is what gives Cole a place to rebuild herself, and her familial connections, post-prison. Despite the fact that the home is decaying—Cole compares it to "an old man with a damp cough"—it is also, as she recognizes at the end, the only legacy of their dead parents (160). It binds the current generation together as the one thing her brother can offer her as partial recompense for failing to visit her in prison: "this home is all we ever had," as she later reflects (161).

Her home and the gentrifying neighborhood around it represent for Cole the contrast between the upwardly mobile and those displaced by their mobility. Riding past the downtown area, she observes, "new metallic apartments jutted into the skyline, mimicking the view of the mountains. Traffic swarmed and coughed under the city's haze and healthy looking young people rode bikes through the streets, past the homeless who curled under wilted cardboard" (154). This contrast provides a metaphor for Cole's own life; she is attuned to the plight of the down-and-out after her years in prison, a no-home home. Cole blames no one but herself for the alcohol-induced mayhem that landed her in prison, but her attention to the misfortunes of others aptly illustrates her awareness of the lack of an equal playing field. Her attention to her nephew, Tomi, may begin out of guilt that she once stole his college fund; it soon becomes motivated, however, by her realization that he lacks most of the basic necessities of childhood. The emphasis on gentrification in this context demonstrates the gaps in privilege that can shape opportunities at an age as early as Tomi's.

One such privilege is access to books. As Cole explores her newly revamped neighborhood where "blond women with high ponytails pushed babies in expensive strollers while white guys in khakis stared at their cellphones," she finds that her childhood home is within walking distance of a bookstore, but not a library (145). Residents, therefore, require money to ride the bus to the library, or more money to purchase books at the bookstore. This real-life geography is also indicative of typical barriers to educational access in many neighborhoods which can be "library deserts" like Cole's. But books are important enough to Cole to invest in acquiring them, and they provide the turning point for both the characters and their creator. The bookstore Cole discovers is likely West Side Books, where Fajardo-Anstine worked on and off for ten years, and which gave her a sense of belonging: "While it was somewhat disorienting to be in my old neighborhood in its new way, I was not disoriented by the books" ("On the 32" 15:36–15:44). By purchasing a book there, and pursuing the series all the way to the nearest library, Tomi and

Cole find a new space together, outside of the deteriorating home and bleak prospects that confine them both. Whether within or outside of prison, books provide Cole a way out of her entrapped space, and a different perspective on her conceptions of home.

"Ghost Sickness," the final story in the collection, again places great weight on moving homes and shifting neighborhoods, in this case by connecting the protagonist's struggle to pass her Western history class with her family's displacement from that very history. Ana Garcia lives in an unairconditioned "one-bedroom brick box" where the streetlamp makes bars of light through the blinds that connote a prison (*Sabrina and Corina* 196). Gentrification has pushed her mother out to the suburbs: "a decade ago, she sold her bungalow on the Northside to a young attorney couple from Philadelphia. They immediately painted the yellow house gray, marking it unrecognizable to anyone from the past. Didn't Louisa Garcia once live here? Wasn't this block the Hispanic or Italian side of town? No one asks questions like this anymore. No one remembers and no one cares" (200). Replacing the brightly colored facade with a dingier tone recalls Cisneros's battle over her purple house, while also emphasizing that gentrifiers paint over memory and history as well as homes. However, the past, like the yellow paint, may lie just beneath the surface. The assertion that no one remembers or cares is undone by the very act of narration, presumably from Ana's perspective; the passage implies that she herself is actively doing both.

Remembering is a central concern of the story, as Ana's scholarship is contingent on her recalling history, and yet "none of the dates stick. Everything blurs" (196). She received this scholarship "given to the grandchildren of Denver residents, mostly Hispano, who once occupied the Westside neighborhood before it was plowed to make way for an urban campus" (197)—yet she seems unable to remember the required facts precisely because she is cut off from this heritage and legacy of land. The encroaching school employs an encroaching professor, an East Coast transplant condescendingly teaching the history of the West and surnamed Brown although she is not. Professor Brown shows clear favoritism to the White students and cannot remember Ana's name—a fact with particular resonance as this story directly follows "All Her Names" and shares its concerns with remembering and recording. Ana still takes one crucial piece of information from the class: the definition for the "ghost sickness" of the title as "a culture-bound syndrome of the Navajo . . . *comes after abrupt/violent death of a loved one*" (203). Brown elaborates that Western medicine diagnoses these symptoms as anxiety or depression (correctly, she implies), and therefore "taken out of its cultural context, the illness doesn't exist" (203). Ghost sickness is thus simultaneously the ghost of a sickness and a sickness caused by ghosts. The death of Ana's free-spirit Navajo boyfriend, Clifton, could presumably cause her ghost sickness, but instead he seems to provide a posthumous healing force. Poised to fail her final exam, Ana notices the sidelined extra credit question on the Navajo origin myth and remembers Clifton's "Diné story, the beginning of it all . . . our story of everything" (208–9). Despite her loss of neighborhood, of heritage, of Clifton himself, the story continues, for Ana knows that "she'd remember every word for the rest of her life" (209). As the neighborhood is lost but the narrative lives on, Fajardo-Anstine closes her collection with themes of place, space, ancestry, and "stories of everything" that will take center stage in her first novel.

WOMAN OF LIGHT: HOME ON THE FRONT RANGE

Fajardo-Anstine claimed her first novel, *Woman of Light*, "began with one question: how did I become so mixed?" ("On the 32" 21:00-21:05). This parallels Cisneros's description of her own writing process in "To Seville, with Love": "And me, hiding out on the border searching for the homeland of the imagination. I've since been filled with a desire to travel somewhere that might explain and answer the question 'Where are you from?' and, in turn, 'Who are you?' Isn't this why all writers write, or is it just those of us who live on borders?" (227). Searching for an understanding of identity and ancestry proved inspirational for both authors. Fajardo-Anstine describes what she uncovered of her border-crossing background in a 2019 interview with *Westword*: "I come from an enormous Wild West Chicano family, a family that is mixed with Filipino, Jewish and Anglo. Our mixture and existence comes out of our place." Location and migration diversify families, which in turn diversify the places they live. *Woman of Light* is born of this alchemy, tracing the central family's origins from Southern Colorado up to Denver, and from Indigenous and Mexican roots to Filipino and Belgian ones. At the time her story begins, Colorado itself is not yet a state, and therefore has no official borders. Yet the novel pays close attention to the characters' more metaphorical border crossings: those between races, classes, and genders.

In setting the primary narrative of her novel in the 1930s, Fajardo-Anstine can display casual, overt, institutionalized racism that serves as a reminder of all that simmers beneath the surface in our present day.[8] Racial borders and boundaries confront Luz Lopez, the protagonist of *Woman of Light*, from the beginning. Walking through a public park, she notices white flyers on trees, "as if a fungus has overrun the bark," that turn out to be signs proclaiming that "This park belongs to WHITE PROTESTANTS: NO GOOKS, SPICS, NIGGERS Allowed" (23). Luz is visibly upset by this sign, yet she is accustomed to being barred from public spaces: "There were many places she had been told she wasn't allowed. Denver Dry Goods, Elitch Gardens, over the dead in Cheesman Park" (99). This casual recitation is, in some ways, even more chilling than the Klan violence that later erupts into her office space, reminding Luz and the reader that even the professional haven where she has gained respect is not safe from racial brutality.

Of all the barred spaces, however, it is perhaps the Rose Dixon library[9]—happy to let dogs in but not Mexicans—which causes Luz the greatest affront. In a sequence reminiscent of a dark fairy tale, Luz must first navigate past intimidating guardian lions "warning her to stay away from their kingdom" (97). The next beastly challenge confronting intrepid library visitors is a mural with bears, wild animals whose capture and abuse once led to tragedy for Luz's grandmother.[10] The mural's inscription, "THE WORLD IS SO FULL OF A NUMBER OF THINGS, I'M SURE WE SHOULD ALL BE AS HAPPY AS KINGS," (97) originally derives from the poem "Happy Thought" in Robert Louis Stevenson's *A Child's Garden of Verses*, but in this context it seems designed to put the poor in their place by implying that happiness is reserved for kings and possessors of things. The librarians themselves, even more imposing gatekeepers than their stone lion sentinels, become the third barrier, denying Luz access to the community board for job ads on the grounds that it is not in Spanish, disregarding the fact that they are conversing in English at the time. They evict her with instructions to seek out her own neighborhood library, to which Luz responds only in her own mind: "*But my neighborhood doesn't have a library*" (99). This moment gestures back to Virginia Woolf's famous description of being denied access to the male-only library at "Oxbridge" in the 1920s. In *A Room of One's Own*, a gatekeeper similar to those at Rose Dixon informs the narrator that "ladies are only admitted to the library if accompanied by a Fellow of the College or furnished with a letter of introduction" (8). Like Luz, Woolf's narrator expresses her objections for the reader's eyes only: "That a famous library has been cursed by a woman is a matter of complete indifference to a famous library" (8). These stories from the past contrast the library that proves lifesaving for present-day Tomi and Cole in *Sabrina and Corina*, who need to take a bus to access it but at least encounter no guardians at the gates. This contrast between then and now emphasizes the importance of keeping knowledge free and accessible to all. Indeed, were she allowed into the library itself, Luz might have been able to discover Virginia Woolf, and even learn that the two-line all-caps poem on the mural was penned by strident anti-colonialist Robert Louis Stevenson, an immigrant who settled in Samoa for the last five years of his life and urged the local population to resist their European oppressors. These contexts, apparent to their contemporary author, are forbidden to her 1930s protagonist along with access to the library and all the opportunities it represents.

Woolf's book begins with the barred library but goes on to argue that, as the title implies, women writers require private space within their own home. Later, bell hooks takes up a similar idea in her 1990 essay, "Homeplace: A Site of Resistance." As discussed, this concept was particularly resonant for Cisneros, who, like Woolf and hooks, sees a home as the ultimate resistance to being locked out, enabling women and people of color space to reflect and dream behind their own locked doors. Jacqueline Doyle discusses this connection in detail, reading Cisneros as a retelling of Woolf, and detailing previous re-readings by others who point out what Woolf missed: notably race (Alice Walker) and class (Tillie Olsen). *Mango Street*, she argues, is a reinterpretation of *Room of One's Own* complicated by these additional concerns of race and class—ones that Woolf, feminist icon though she may be, tends to overlook. Doyle notes that Esperanza's longed-for dream home serves various functions: "Esperanza's 'house of my own' simultaneously represents an escape from the barrio, a rejection of the domestic drudgery of 'home' . . . a solitary space for her creativity, and a communal expression of women's lives" (22). All this is encapsulated, for Cisneros, in the image of home, which is a through-line not only for the stories of *Mango Street*, but for most of her other work as well. *Woman of Light*, however, complicates this emphasis on the physical space of home as a prerequisite to creativity.

Physical houses and property ownership may be less crucial to *Woman of Light* as a reflection of the Lopez family's Native American roots. Luz's grandfather Pidre believes that "no human being can possess land," (245) a tenet quickly challenged when Anglos discover radium mines on his property. The historically inevitable occurs, and Pidre is robbed of a claim he didn't believe he had, but this theft is not the focus of the family story. While the land loss could be the original trauma for the Lopez line, it instead becomes secondary to the successive parent loss occurring throughout the generations. Grandfather Pidre is killed by the land thieves, but only after his impetuous friend draws his weapon on them; and while he is the first of his family to leave his children behind, he is not the last. The land theft scene occurs only near the novel's close, whereas both the opening and final scenes focus on the adoption of orphans and the construction of a family. In between, each successive generation finds itself abandoned through choice, mental illness, or death. In other words, parent loss, not land loss, becomes the original and cyclically repeated sin.[11]

Three decades after her grandfather loses his land and his life, Luz shares a crowded one-bedroom apartment with her brother and aunt. The building, with the angry and incongruous name Hornet Moon, reeks of carcasses from the butcher in the alley and contains broken appliances and a radiator their landlord refuses to fix. Luz privately fumes, "Why didn't they deserve heat? They had paid their rent, struggled for it with pawned necklaces and traded furniture and hands scrubbed raw cleaning white women's bloody clothes" (88). Luz's work as a laundress, like so many low-income occupations, brings her intimately close to the wealthy, making her increasingly aware of the discrepancies between her life and theirs. As she visits the lavish Victorian homes of her clients, Luz "felt locked out, and wondered why she even wanted in" (21). This again recalls Woolf's *Room of One's Own*, in which the narrator reflects upon being barred admission to all Oxbridge has to offer: "I thought how unpleasant it is to be locked out; and I thought how it is worse, perhaps, to be locked in" (24). Luz's co-worker and cousin, Lizette, makes a similar observation when she comes upon a "Queen Anne mansion" and observes its "encapsulating iron gate with murderous spikes, either to keep people out or keep them in" (213). Upon discovering that those housed within are unwed and unwanted pregnant White women, Lizette is happy to be on the outside, feeling "grateful that she didn't come from a people so unbearable as to hide their own women away when they believed them full of unfavorable babies" (217). In conversation with Luz, she similarly valorizes her outcast identity position, observing that the lives of the rich are dull in comparison and that the fancy facades of their homes are merely "how they trick themselves into thinking they're better than we are" (21). Lizette, like Virginia Woolf before her, insists on the potential for pride in remaining on the outside.

Lizette's desires are complex, however, and although she may scoff at the Victorian mansions, she, like Esperanza, dreams of "a big white house that was all her own" (212). Luz reads this house in her predictive tea leaves as a less imposing one than the mansions they pass, seeing her cousin's future in "a sunny apartment with a yellow kitchen, white French doors, brick walls" (7). For Lizette, both house and husband are essential components of her eventual maturity. She chooses a kind man, and she seems poised to avoid the type of violent or stifling marriage that entraps so many of the characters previously discussed. Instead, Lizette happily moves with her husband to "a two-bedroom home to rent on Inca street[12] that had a square yard and a blossoming peach tree" (227). They are still tenants, not owners, and this house has a blue kitchen rather than the yellow one Luz foresees, so it appears to be the first step towards "a life of her own" as she imagines it, separate from the child-riddled space of her fertile and harried parents (210). Lizette, then, achieves the dream of a separate space that Cisneros's Esperanza so desperately imagined, and apparently without the sacrifices made by characters like Sally to achieve it.

Lizette, however, is a reflection and refraction of Luz, her *prima hermana,* or a cousin as close as a sister. The two are mirror images of each other, both parallels and opposites: "Sometimes, when Luz looked at Lizette, it was as if she were peering into a speckled mirror at pieces of herself rearranged in another person. It was her shyness distorted into assertiveness and her delicate features pulled into the beauty of masculine femininity" (226). Sabrina and Corina, in Fajardo-Anstine's first collection, are *primas hermanas* as well, and likewise are described with the imagery of mirrors: "All around we were reflected in the four mirrors endlessly, like one tangled spider of a girl" (30). In both cases the narrative focuses on the quieter, more centered, and more ambitious of the pair, Sabrina and Luz, respectively, each using the cousin as contrast. It is through Luz's perspective, therefore, that we see a movement away from a desire for the physical space to define home, and towards a sense of familial community instead.

The novel concludes by gesturing back to the first scene, when the original orphan's great-granddaughter follows his path: like Pidre, she is abandoned, discovered, and finally given a home. The ending revises the beginning, for instead of an older woman adopting an unknown boy, the father reclaims his own daughter, bringing her into the found-family of women who choose not to marry: his sister, their aunt, and her girlfriend, Ethel. We do not learn if this chosen family remains in the aunt's apartment, meat-reeking and heat-seeking, or if they relocate to the higher-class Eastside with Ethel. For a book (and a writer) so concerned with space, carefully describing buildings and naming streets, this seems at first an odd omission. However, Fajardo-Anstine focuses on neighborhoods, rather than individual residences, as a determination of home. The climax in this interpretation is the middle of the novel, not the end, when Luz's eventual lover teaches her ten-year-old self to claim her environs as her own: "'THIS IS MY CITY!' They yelled together until their voices boomed, high and arching, rattling streetcar cables and smoggy windows, soaring between stone tenements and factory tufts. This, she repeated, is ours" (151). This remains one of the most triumphant moments of Luz's life, and one that informs her identity apart from all those who try to impose it upon her. No gatekeepers will bar her from the life she has chosen as her own. Wherever they reside, the family of five has found each other, and claimed the city for their own; their house itself becomes a place of lesser importance.

CONCLUSION: WRITING IN/OF COMMUNITY

Sandra Cisneros speaks often and generously of the collaborative nature of her work. Michelle Tokarczyk observes that "although Dickinson's work was an inspiration to Cisneros, her life was a cautionary tale. The nineteenth-century author was far more removed from ordinary people that Cisneros ever wanted to be" (106). In fact, connecting with people was the source of inspiration for much of her work, as well as solace to her soul. In "*The House on Mango Street*'s Tenth Birthday" Cisneros expresses gratitude to her students for some of the stories that eventually became Esperanza's: "Because I often felt helpless as a teacher and a counselor to alter their lives, their stories began to surface in my 'memoir'; then *Mango Street* no longer was my story, but became all our stories . . . I gathered different parts of other people's lives to create a story like a collage" (129). In her essay "Resurrections," she observes of her latest novella, *Have You Seen Marie*, that "this book became a collective community effort" (301). Kali Fajardo-Anstine's work becomes part of this larger collaborative project. *Woman of Light* has a chapter entitled "Three Sisters," and like *Mango Street*'s chapter of the same name, it involves three mysterious sisters who appear for a single significant conversation with the protagonist before vanishing forever. The very first story in Fajardo-Anstine's first collection is set in a "small purple house"—perhaps one more subtle form of tribute to her literary foremother. The conversation between these two writers is clear, as is their shared belief that all writing is in some ways collaborative. This commitment to gathering stories otherwise untold, remaking them, and sharing them with the world counters standard monological forms of writing and provides a voice for "the ones who cannot out" (*Mango Street* 110). We see, once again, that novels are not "solitary births" (Woolf 65) but complex acts of communication and collaboration. Cisneros has always drawn from her community to create her art—an art, of course, which in turn gave back to the community.

Cisneros expands this idea further through her participation in the broader art community of sculptors, painters, performers, and activists in San Antonio. Cisneros credits the art scene there as "terrifically inclusive," praising how it "brought down the apartheid walls of class, color, and sexuality existent in San Antonio for generations" ("Infinito Botánica" 215). She specifically praises the local aesthetic of *rascuache*, or art put together from anything at hand (216). While the concept is similar to the French term *bricolage,* coined by anthropologist Claude Lévi-Strauss, Cisneros uses a term derives from the indigenous Nahuatl, preserving the spelling over the Anglicized *rasquache*. The word is, significantly, an insult reclaimed, originating as a way of scoffing at the poor but later becoming a celebrated art form. The writing of Cisneros and Fajardo-Anstine can be compared to *rascuache* in the visual arts; both chose to piece together stories from experiences—their own and that of others—from their humble backgrounds and transform them into timeless and critically lauded pieces of art.

For Fajardo-Anstine, many of these fragments came from her own family history of hardship. Elizabeth Hernandez describes her process of including many of these painful family tales of abandonment, discrimination, and poverty: "The stories were passed down through her family in the oral tradition—rich histories archived by tongue, ear and memory—but Fajardo-Anstine's fingers itched to preserve them in ink" ("This Highly Anticipated").

Fajardo-Anstine weaves together these family narratives in a way that calls attention to some of the more colorful moments in her familial history while also creating her own original story. The novel brings, for example, Native American prophets and the ghosts of Catholic priests together within the first few pages, conversing across time and over the barriers of life and death. In deciding to "preserve them in ink," Fajardo-Anstine finds a way to make, as her epigraph quotes from *The Tempest*, the past into prologue.

This, then, is one of the most crucial similarities between Cisneros and Fajardo-Anstine: The works of these authors share an understanding that the written space is one that can preserve all these communities that have contributed to their making, simultaneously fixed on the page and fluid in their impact on readers. Esperanza becomes a writer, Luz becomes the keeper of family lore, and characters throughout "Sabrina and Corina" show themselves to be adept storytellers. In telling the stories of these storytellers, the authors bring their readers into their communities and demonstrate the necessity of doing so. In *House on Mango Street* Aunt Lupe encourages Esperanza to continue writing not because it is enjoyable, lucrative, or cathartic, but because "It will keep you free" (61). The repetition of "keep" in place of the expected cliches—"set you free" or "make you free"—emphasizes that Esperanza already has the freedom she seeks, as evinced by the writing we see before us on the page, but that she must work to maintain it for herself and, presumably, others. Similarly, Fajardo-Anstine observes, "My family doesn't let stories disappear . . . That's why I'm a storyteller, too, because I knew how important it was to keep them alive, but I also would meet other people from my background who didn't have access to all their stories. It is really important to me to retain cultural stories" (Hernandez, "This Highly Anticipated"). In writing them down she both preserves them and, through fiction, remakes them in her own way for future generations.

Revising historical misconceptions is, in fact, part of Fajardo-Anstine's explicit project. As she explained in an interview about *Women of Light*, her objective for the book is quite ambitious: "So much of our identity as a Western space has been defined by the cowboy narrative, the myth of the stoic outlawed cowboy figure. This is going to be the first time somebody is coming to the West in a way that is not the stereotype mythology" (Athena). Within the novel itself, she elaborates on the idea of undoing the cowboy mythology, and on the importance of retelling stories in a new way. Just before he meets the woman who will redefine his own life story, Luz's Native American grandfather, Pidre, reflects, "Anglos were perhaps the most dangerous storytellers of all—for they believed only their own words, and they allowed their stories to trample the truths of nearly every other man on Earth" (73). *Woman of Light* undoes this narrative injustice by ensuring that the family story will move forward, told by and to those whom it most concerns.

The novel's final passages describe Luz passing the family history down to her niece: "Now, go on, tell her our stories," her brother prompts (304). Luz chooses, in the last line, to begin with the beginning of the novel: the story of her grandfather's adoption, the root of her own family tree. In writing down her own family stories but remaking them into fiction, Fajardo-Anstine ensures her truths will not be trampled; instead, her novel allows each history to be told and retold, far beyond the limits of one family or even one community. For these writers, storytelling itself is the crucial action.

To conclude where this chapter began, Cherríe Moraga states, "One voice is not enough, nor two, although this is where dialogue begins. . . . The real power, as you and I well know, is collective" ("La Güera" 29). Cisneros and Fajardo-Anstine create a dialogue to which readers and future writers must add their own voices for collective empowerment. One author like Sandra Cisneros begets many more like Kali Fajardo-Anstine, who will continue to influence future generations of readers, writers, and activists to come.

NOTES

1. I use the contemporary gender-neutral "Latine," whereas Cisneros in the following quotation uses "Latinos and Latinas." Other common terms include "Latinx" (also gender-neutral, but unpronounceable in Spanish), and the older term "Hispanic," which references all Spanish speakers rather than people of Central and South American heritage, as I intend here. Terminology adapts as people do, so I write this knowing that Latine may be soon be replaced by something more current/specific as well.

2. Celeste Ng expresses a similar sentiment in *Salon,* explaining that during her book tour for *Everything I Never Told You* she was often told that "there aren't that many of you": "I heard it enough to realize that even many serious readers—the kind of people who come to author readings on gorgeous summer evenings—just can't name any Asian American women writers beyond the phenomenally well-known Amy Tan."

3. Cisneros states that her path to Catholic school was influenced by neighborhood and class rather than religion: "I went to Catholic school not because my parents were devout but because there wasn't an alternative to getting your kids an education and not getting them beat up in the schoolyard" (qtd. in Torres 195).

4. Rooted yet free, Esperanza, like Pilate Dead, can fly without leaving the ground. See Chapter Three for more on this comparison.

5. Both authors are on the older end as well, though with slightly different dynamics: Fajardo-Anstine is the second of seven with only one male, and Cisneros the third of seven with only one female.

6. Chapter three discusses the privileging of houses over people in connection to plantations and the legacy of slavery.

7. Notably, Alicia, passing into her new White world, easily sweet-talks her way out of a police encounter despite the incriminating cans of spray paint; the working-class

narrator of "Tomi" is not so lucky. See Chapter Three for Jesmyn Ward's depiction of racial profiling by police.

8. Celeste Ng similarly uses her 1970s timeframe in *Everything I Never Told You* to depict more overt racism towards her Chinese characters, as discussed in Chapter Two.

9. No library by this name currently exists in Denver, so, unlike many of Fajardo-Anstine's locations, it appears to be fictional.

10. A black bear also appears in Ana Garcia's vision foretelling her boyfriend's death in "Ghost Sickness" (*Sabrina and Corina* 205).

11. This parallels the Dead family as discussed in Chapter Three; while Macon Dead I dies defending his land, it is abandoning his children that proves the enduring family trauma.

12. Inca Street references another indigenous civilization of the Americas, and, like Galapago Street, is one where Fajardo-Anstine herself resided—in this case, during college (Hernandez, "Highly Anticipated").

Chapter Five

Literary Remix

It's the admission that we're part of something, that when we're alone writing we're not alone—that the imaginative life and real life intertwine.

—Maxine Hong Kingston, "Coming Home"

INTERTEXTUALITIES REVISITED

This book has both made a case for, and modeled the process of, reading across and between texts as a means of creating radical empathy. When we perceive novels only as isolated events, as discrete objects between two covers, we lose sight of the rich intertextuality that forged them and of their potential to create new literary conversations. The pairings here of a canonical female author of color with a later one she influenced, along with significant intertexts along the way, attempt to emphasize some such connections in hopes that they will lead to more. Reading deeply and broadly in this way is the first step towards an empathic understanding of the injustices of the world, and towards motivating us to take action against them.

This final chapter is something of a literary remix, returning to the authors and themes already discussed and moving across the chapters to suggest possibilities for new conversations and across racial divides. The overlapping of influences and motifs apparent in this reshuffling demonstrates that many of these works are branches on the same literary tree. Sandra Cisneros eloquently describes this metaphor when writing about the influence *A Tree Grows in Brooklyn* had on her mother as a young girl, and how that book about a young girl struggling to grow up in a working-class neighborhood impacted her in turn:

Betty Smith writing about growing up poor, growing up ashamed because she
was poor, sheltered my mother when she was a young woman trying to find her
way from poverty and shame out to her true home. I am kin of Betty Smith, and
Betty Smith is kin of Thomas Wolfe, and so we are branches of the same tree.
Your people are my people, whither thou goest, me too. (*House of My Own* 39)

This passage reaches back to the Bible for its terminology ("kin,") and its
specific reference to Ruth 1:16–17 at the end; yet Cisneros weaves in her own
visible thread with the reference to a "true home," her work's major theme,
and through the simple, colloquial conclusion: "me too." In those two words
Cisneros asserts herself, in her own voice, as part of the longstanding literary
lineage that expands kinship to include those related to us not only by blood-
lines but by the lines on a page.

   One root of the family tree shared by the writers discussed here is William
Faulkner, whose substantial contributions to the concept of radical empathy I
discussed in Chapter One. His insistence on the impact of communal history
as determined by our cultural, historical, racial, economic, and familial pasts
foreshadows later theories of intersectionality and Critical Race Theory, and
thus resonates with much of the work of the authors discussed here. His influ-
ence on most of these writers is direct and traceable. Celeste Ng describes
how Hannah savors her stolen copy of Lydia's assigned text, *The Sound and
the Fury*. Toni Morrison wrote her master's thesis on Faulkner and published
an essay "On Faulkner and Women" in her final collection. Jesmyn Ward
mentions Faulkner as a particular influence due to her Mississippi heritage,
and whole conferences are being dedicated to comparing their work. Despite
the very real-life city of Denver that provides the setting for much of her
work, Kali Fajardo-Anstine was also inspired by Faulkner's invented com-
munity: "You know, Faulkner has his fictional Yoknapatawpha County . . . I
have the landscape of the Lost Territory in my mind, but because my family
left that place, I thought it would be more respectful to render it as a fictional
space" (Luna). And without quoting Faulkner directly, Sandra Cisneros uses a
metaphor very similar to Faulkner's own (see p. 16) in her essay *¡Que Vivan
Los Colores!*: "If the universe is a cloth, then all humanity is interwoven
with different colored threads. Pull one string, and the whole cloth comes
undone . . . Each person who comes into your life affects your *destino*, and
you affect theirs" (171). In short, Faulkner is one thread in a conversation
that each of these authors is having—with him, with each other, and with
their readers.

   To continue to pull a few more of these threads, we should consider that
these writers have myriad connections to one another beyond those already
discussed within each individual chapter. Sandra Cisneros claimed that the
opening chapter of Maxine Hong Kingston's *Woman Warrior*, "No Name

Woman," provided the initial inspiration for "My Name," one of the first vignettes in *The House on Mango Street* (Quintana 363). Her revision shows increased hope for female agency: Esperanza both names herself ("Lisandra or Maritza or Zeze the X") and, eventually, owns her given name, in contrast to Kingston's aunt whose name is lost to history (11). In her book on Cisneros, Eilidh AB Hall elaborates on these connections to Kingston:

> The explicit connection between Hong Kingston's work and Cisneros' . . . traces a shared motherline between women of colour of many cultures and ethnicities in the United States. Although each such story is unique, there is a connection through the motherline . . . In the works of writers like Cisneros, Castillo, Hong Kingston, and Walker, the sympathetic vibrations connecting them are as a result of their positions as women of colour writing stories from a place at the margin of mainstream U.S. literary and cultural society. (176)

The "shared motherline" links each of the authors discussed here, as each one has "sympathetic vibrations" connecting her to the others. Hall adds other writers, Walker and Castillo, to the list, and of course other readers would add more, and so the connections across time and ethnicities grow.

While comparisons like these between writers of different racial backgrounds have become more popular in recent years, such connections have long existed within the fictional works themselves. Jayson T. Gonzales Sae-Saue delves into some of the often-overlooked inter-ethnic moments in the foundational texts by women of color that I have discussed here. He pays particular attention to the scene at the end of *Woman Warrior* when Kingston's mother works in the tomato fields with Mexican-American women: "The mother's stories of Asian, Asian American, Mexican, and Mexican American women sending monies to their respective 'villages' foster within the narrator a self-awareness which extends beyond ethnic boundaries and crosses US national borders, anticipating the inter-ethnic focus of the novel's finale and the transnational future of Asian American literature in general" (272). This brief moment of cultural exchange demonstrates how Kingston's Chinese American family empathically understands the experience of Mexican American women, linked by labor. Its inclusion in Kingston's autobiographical memoir implies a broader potential for cross-cultural conversations that imagine similarities in seemingly disparate experiences.

Similarly, when Cisneros writes in "My Name" that Esperanza, like her great-grandmother, has a birthday in the "Chinese year of the horse," we may perceive a link between the emerging feminist identity of Esperanza and that of young Kingston as portrayed in her memoir. Esperanza elaborates on the meaning of her birth year, and then contradicts it, claiming the year of the horse "is supposed to be bad luck if you're born female—but I think this is a Chinese lie because the Chinese, like Mexicans, don't like their women strong" (11). This mention of another ethnicity is notable for a narrator whose life seems entirely conscribed by her Latine neighborhood. Sae-Saue writes of this moment that although "there are no Asian characters . . . Esperanza's encounter with the Chinese zodiac calendar gestures to how divergent populations interact through crisscrossing trajectories of *cultural traffic*" (276). In effect, Sae-Saue makes an argument for the importance of radical empathy through cultural products, like books: Esperanza may only interact with Latine people, but she experiences an empathic feminist moment with Chinese women through her understanding of their zodiac. She connects imaginatively to Chinese women even though she may never have encountered one.

Just as Cisneros' "My Name" chapter, and possibly her Chinese Zodiac allusion, nod towards Kingston, Kingston explicitly connects the opening line of her first book ("You must not tell anyone") back to the opening line of Morrison's first book. As she told Angels Carabí in an interview: "Yes, 'Don't tell, don't tell.' This beginning has a connection with Morrison. She starts her book *The Bluest Eye* with 'Quiet as it is kept.'" Both books open by demanding a silence that the novels themselves break. Sae-Saue further notes the connection between Kingston's narrator and her young Black friend who imitates her "Shanghai-style" hairdo: "the voice that the narrator celebrates at the end of the novel develops from a childhood experience in which she and an African American girl imagine a powerful Afro-Chinese inter-subjective of mind and body" (271). He further discusses the importance of identifying with someone of a different heritage without seeking to become that person, praising "the narrator's power to imagine a 'Negro' identity relative to her own while respecting ethnic distinctions" (272). Kingston's narrator admires aspects of her Black friend's culture while simultaneously celebrating and sharing her own.[1] Finally, Kingston and Morrison developed a personal connection after the publications of *Woman Warrior* and *Song of Solomon* in the 1970s. Both celebrated writers by this point, Kingston, Morrison, and a few other lauded literati traveled to China together in 1984 for a conference entitled "The Sources of Creativity." In 2011, they reunited and discussed their previous trip at the 92 Street Y, inspiring Kingston to compare their writing processes: "Toni sees a painting when she writes . . . She sees lines of red over there and green and blue dots up here and white down there. That's how she works, that's how I work" (Cheney). Laguna author Leslie Marmon Silko attended both the 1984 conference in China and the 2011 reunion with the two of them. Were she to describe her writing process, she might well find echoes with both of these women writers of color, and perhaps with others as well, and so the branches of the literary tree continue to spread.

READING ACROSS COLOR LINES

Each chapter so far has defied the "Single Story" by exploring complex views of a given topic from each ethnicity, ensuring that no author is viewed in isolation or as the sole representative of a group. This section demonstrates how each intersectionally focused theme applied to one ethnic group above can easily cross over and apply to the others. By bringing our previous authors into new conversations, we read each more deeply and avoid isolating ethnic categories from each other. The result suggests the many ways we can expand our narrative understanding by reading both within *and* across color lines.

To begin, we may apply the silencing stereotype from chapter two to the bilingual characters in chapter four. Children of immigrants across ethnic groups may both struggle with and embrace the process of moving between different linguistic worlds, often requiring English in school but the parents' native language at home. Fatima Mujcinovic discusses the importance of incorporating bilingualism into fiction for second-generation writers, including those analyzed here:

> Minority authors like Kingston and Cisneros recognize that inserting marks of otherness into the English language enables them to present the uniqueness of their ethnic traditions while also claiming their place in America's culture and language. This conscious process of adapting dominant literacy to create new literary models reflects a democratic understanding of culture, elucidating the need for inclusive and diverse literacy practices in multicultural societies. (99)

Inclusive literacy allows readers to enter the linguistic worlds of the authors. Monolingual readers stumped by the occasional Spanish word in *The House on Mango Street*, for example, are invited to relate to the experience of the immigrant characters who speak no English, such as Mamacita. Initially described with a florid appearance of "fuchsia roses and green perfume," Mamacita gradually diminishes in the course of her short vignette (*Mango Street* 76). Possessing only eight English words, she is self-silenced by her longing to remain, linguistically at least, in her home country. Esperanza theorizes that this lack of language is what keeps her locked in her room, saying first that "she doesn't come out because she is afraid to speak English," and then shifting that phrase slightly to say she is "afraid of English" itself (77). The change in wording suggests that Mamacita's fears have "bloomed," "huge, enormous," just as she herself blooms out of the cab that conveys her to her prison/home on Mango Street (77). The story acknowledges, and even respects, these fears by demonstrating the power of language. Three of Mamacita's eight words are "no speak English," a phrase she typically employs as a defense; at the end of the vignette, however, she uses it as a command to her son, ordering him to cease speaking in the language of her non-home. Cisneros gives the phrase a third turn as the chapter title, as though Esperanza's framing of the tale implies her own commentary on the importance of language. Indeed, Esperanza's ever-evocative style shows the same; while Mamacita mutely mourns for home, Esperanza gives color to her longing, vividly describing Mamacita's former residence as "pink as hollyhocks with lots of startled light" (77). Esperanza understands Mamacita more than bilingually; she reads her empathically, and as such can translate her experience to the wider world. The very potential to translate into different languages and modes renders multilingual works complex and nuanced rather than "untranslatable," as some may assume.

Kingston explains her own work in a way that parallels Cisneros' well: "There are puns for Chinese speakers only, and I do not point them out for non-Chinese speakers. There are some visual puns best appreciated by those who write Chinese. I've written jokes in that book so private, only I can get them" ("Cultural Mis-readings" 65). This linguistic originality is, I would argue, *more* inclusive, in that it provides an empathic entry point for a wide variety of readers.

While most of Fajardo-Anstine's characters are fluent in English, their identity positions can lead them into the culturally enforced silencing we saw in Celeste Ng's work. In "Sisters," Fajardo-Anstine envisions a lesbian character inspired by a real-life one in her family history who must hide her sexuality due to the pervasive homophobia of the 1950s. When a spurned suitor suspects Doty's secret he beats her blind, ensuring her ongoing silence and complicity in his narrative; when a woman later expresses concern for, and perhaps interest in her, Doty repeats her attacker's version: "I had an accident," she says, adding even more grimly, "no one says anything about it at all" (69). Doty and the many other women silenced through death in *Sabrina and Corina* are countered by the women who live on and will tell their stories. In a sense the whole collection is filled with Sabrinas and/or Corinas, victims and survivor/narrators, paralleling the dynamic between the drowned women in both Kingston's and Ng's works and the narrators who tell their tales. I would argue that this pattern continues in *Woman of Light*. Emma Athena calls attention to the silencing aspect in her review of the novel: "as the women grow farther from their pre-Anglo matriarch, the Sleepy Prophet of the Lost Territory, their voices weaken." She cites a vivid image of Luz's voicelessness around a love interest: "she'd open her mouth to speak but could only picture white moths fluttering from her lips" (*Woman of Light* 228). While there are moments like these when the voices of each woman falter in the face of oppression, they do gain strength as the novel progresses, and, notably, the final pages are filled with Luz's narrations as she gives a full accounting to her found-family: her cousin, her aunt, and her brother's reclaimed daughter. Like Kingston and Ng, she speaks across generations.

Silencing, both linguistic and gendered, has multiple similarities in these Chinese and Chicana works. Masculinity, however, may look quite different across racial lines; the stereotypes discussed for the Black male protagonists in Chapter Three look different for the Asian male characters in Chapter Two, and may look more different still when recounted by women authors. Kingston's *China Men* attempted to counterbalance *The Woman Warrior* by taking the perspective of her male ancestors, much as *Song of Solomon* seems to be Morrison's male-centered answer to her previous novel of female friendship, *Sula*. In both cases, however, the feminist strain tends to dominate. While ostensibly telling the story of men, both potently underscore the plight of women. For example, Morrison delivers a brutal take-down of her main character through the voice of his sister, Lena, who taunts him: "but now you know what's best for the very woman who wiped the dribble from your chin because you were too young to know how to spit" (215). Similarly, in recounting one myth Kingston has her gods decree: "This man is too wicked to be reborn a man. Let him be born a woman," clearly critiquing the paternalistic structure that pervades even the mythology she has been taught since childhood (*China Men* 120).

Stereotypes emasculating Chinese men have been culturally pervasive, as seen in the Chapter Two discussion connecting the works of Frank Chin with James's consistent gender anxieties in *Everything I Never Told You*. As Chin writes in "Confessions of a Chinatown Cowboy," Chinese American men were subject to different, but no less damaging, gender stereotypes than most other groups, for "unlike the white stereotype of the evil black stud, Indian rapist, Mexican macho," Asian men, he argues, are "lovable for being a race of sissies, cowed by women" (95). This explicit contrast to other groups commonly vilified as sexually threatening demonstrates the differences between James's evolving understanding of his own masculinity and that of the Black male protagonists in Morrison and Ward. Chin goes on to observe that "The stereotype of us being a race without manhood has been so thoroughly and subtly suffused throughout American culture for so long that it's become a comfortable part of the American subconscious" (99). In fact, he explicitly blames Kingston as a perpetrator in this culture, accusing her of furthering extant negative stereotypes of Chinese males. Edward Iwata summarizes their literary feud: "The 'Angry Man' persona is the key to Chin's manhood and complexity. Chin thinks each bold word of his, each righteous act, will save his Asian America from the hated stereotypes, from death by assimilation— and from Maxine Hong Kingston." He goes on to state, rather dramatically, that "the struggle between Chin and Kingston is a literary battle for the soul of Asian America." If so, this struggle reaches its climax in Kingston's first novel, *Tripmaster Monkey: His Fake Book.*

Tripmaster Monkey, previously discussed in the introduction, features a male protagonist who resembles Chin himself: a volatile playwright preoccupied by both his Chinese American and male identity positions. Inhabiting a fictionalized version of her most vocal critic's mindset for the duration of her novel is, in itself, an act of radical empathy parallel to what Morrison and Ward achieve through the Black male protagonists in their novels. In fact, Kingston goes beyond mere inclusion and powerfully reconciles Wittman's desired masculinity with her own pacifism. She accomplishes this in part via a third person omniscient female narrator, Kuan Yin, goddess of mercy. As she describe in an interview with Marilyn Chin, "In the *Monkey* story, [. . .] Kuan Yin takes a rock and throws it on top of the monkey for 500 years[.] I felt that as narrator I took a rock and threw it on top of the protagonist and captured him. And kept him in place" (88). True to form, Kingston revises this aggressive image, certain to aggravate Chin by incorporating the very type of mythic revisioning he abhors, into a kindlier one within the same interview. Rather than viewing her novel as a prison for her enemy, Kingston generously observes of the real-life Frank Chin: "It's like him sending me hate mail, and I send him love letters, it's like that" (Marilyn Chin 81). *Tripmaster Monkey* does seem more of a love letter than a stony confinement; Wittman is paranoid and volatile but also engaging, compassionate, and funny. Kingston's gentle mocking of her Chin-stand-in through his obsessive concerns over how others perceive him evolves by the end into respect for both the character and his theatrical production: "our monkey, master of change, staged a fake war, which might very well be displacing some real war" (306). Kingston, like Morrison and Ward, looks to the past to understand the future; myths from her cultural heritage become part of her plea for peace in times to come. In her novel's conclusion, the tension between Chin's masculinity and her feminism is overcome by affection: "Dear American monkey, don't be afraid. Here, let us tweak your ear, and kiss your other ear" (340). Kingston wrote in a 1976 letter to Chin, "If I am to grow at all as a writer and a person, I have to wrestle with an understanding about men and write about them/you" (Iwata). This closely parallels Morrison's origin point for writing *Song of Solomon,* as she wondered after her father's death, "what are the men you have known really like?" (xii). Kingston returns to Wittman multiple times in later works (*The Fifth Book of Peace, I Love a Broad Margin to My Life*); one of Morrison's final books, *Home*, returns to the male perspective in considering the trauma of a war veteran. This suggests that both authors might perceive the process of reaching towards "understanding about men" and what they are "really like" challenging, valuable, and lifelong.

Finally, the economic concerns for neighborhood and community from Chapter Four resonate with some of the African American writers in Chapter Three. In his essay "Fifth Avenue, Uptown," James Baldwin describes the challenges of upward mobility for Black people in Harlem: "Anyone who has ever struggled with poverty knows how extremely expensive it is to be poor; and if one is a member of a captive population, economically speaking, one's feet have simply been placed on the treadmill forever . . . The people who have managed to get off this block have only got as far as a more respectable ghetto" (62). He goes on to describe the zero-sum game that is Manhattan real estate, detailing how the very same Fifth Avenue that hosts the most upscale shops in midtown deteriorates into dereliction in Harlem. His summation of the process of ghettoization carries implications of its inevitability: "The pressure within the ghetto causes the ghetto walls to expand, and this expansion is always violent . . . the white people fall back bitterly before the black horde; the landlords make a tidy profit by raising the rent, chopping up rooms, and all but dispensing with the upkeep; and what has once been a neighborhood turns into a 'turf'" (68). This contrasts with the focus on gentrification discussed in chapter four, particularly in Fajardo-Anstine's work, in which urban neighborhoods gain wealth only by pushing people of color further into the outskirts. Both ghettoization and gentrification alike threaten neighborhoods and exacerbate racial segregation.

Song of Solomon opens with a reference to shifting racial demographics, and although the theme is not a prominent one thereafter, it does set the stage for the tensions to come. After the startling announcement of Robert Smith's suicide note, the narrative backs up and slows down to explain why the street on which he plans and performs his fatal leap is called "Not Doctor Street": it is a neighborhood-wide mockery of the White community's attempt to impose their official title, "Mains Avenue," over and against the Black community's colloquial "Doctor Street," a reminder of when one lone black man, the only Black doctor, lived there. "White flight" has evidently altered Southside's racial composition, and the street that Dr. Foster integrated has no White residents remaining. Morrison describes how in her hometown of Lorain, Ohio, segregation was subtle: The ushers in the movie theaters would direct people to seating by color, or the ice cream shop would encourage Black people to order and leave—but such rules were not legally enforceable ("Segregation"). In her novels, prominent White characters appear only rarely; as in the works of Zora Neale Hurston, the Black communities appear largely self-contained. The opening foreshadows that Dr. Foster's grandson, Milkman, will never fully fit in with his neighbors. Instead, he will be forever isolated by his privilege and detached from the residents, only finding a community and legacy far afield.

The characters in Morrison's first novel, *The Bluest Eye*, do not share Milkman's privilege, and the descriptions of neighborhood in Lorain, Ohio, are more closely reminiscent of those from Cisneros and Fajardo-Anstine. Mirroring much from Morrison's childhood, the book depicts de facto segregation when the young Black girls look longingly at the manicured "whites only" park they know not to enter. Their lower-income and predominantly Black community[2] experiences a "hunger for property, for ownership" (18). Like both Cisneros and Fajardo-Anstine, Morrison notes the particular pride that the citizens take in their homes: "Propertied black people spent all their energies, all their love, on their nests. Like frenzied, desperate birds, they overdecorated everything; fussed and fidgeted over their hard-won homes; canned, jellied, and preserved all summer to fill the cupboards and shelves; they painted, picked, and poked at every corner of their houses" (18). The comparison to frenetic birds suggests the homeowners' collective anxiety that they are never far from being "outdoors," or permanently unhoused; furthermore, all their love is "spent," like non-renewable currency, hinting at the lethal neglect of their hatchlings. Pecola Breedlove, living exposed in a former storefront converted to a rental home, never has a chance to find her wings. As the end of the novel makes clear, everyone in Pecola's community bears some responsibility for leaving her forever "outdoors," for expecting her to thrive deprived of both nest and nurture. Pecola's tragic fate demonstrates the need for the shelter of home and community for those who are "a minority in both caste and class" and thus live ever "on the hem of life" (17). Her friends, Claudia and Frieda, are likewise poor, Black, young, and female, but they have a place in the neighborhood and are never at risk of being without a home.

Finally, Ward's setting is more rural but similarly monoracial and threatened by poverty. Her hometown, DeLisle, inspired her slightly fictionalized version, Bois Sauvage, the setting for all three of her novels. Before being renamed for a French settler, DeLisle was called "Wolf Town," as Ward explains in her memoir: "When people ask me about my hometown, I tell them it was called after a wolf before it was partially tamed and settled. I want to impart something of its wild roots, its early savagery" (*Men We Reaped* 9). The town's "savagery" thus reads as a kind of resistance against the colonialism of the French; Ward's invented name, Bois Sauvage, combines both legacies by using the French term for the more genial-sounding "Wild Wood" and thus implicitly retaining the "savagery." The community that Ward brings to light suffers from poverty and lack of social mobility; her first novel, *Where the Line Bleeds*, painstakingly demonstrates how few opportunities await even its promising young men. Despite this fact, however, Ward's second novel, *Salvage the Bones*, argues that this same community is worth preserving; as Greg Chase writes, we can see in her works "the enduring strength of interpersonal and communal bonds in Bois Sauvage" (203). The community's survival proves remarkable in the devastating wake of Hurricane Katrina. Ward explains in the Afterword that *Salvage the Bones* was a rejoinder to the many outsiders who criticized residents who didn't evacuate: "I lived through it. It was terrifying and I needed to write about it. I was also angry at the people who blamed survivors for staying and for choosing to return" (*Salvage the Bones* 263). Although Ward's main characters, like the author and her family, survive, the physical neighborhood doesn't: "Every house had faced the hurricane, and every house had lost" (242). Yet we see Esch and Skeeter from *Salvage the Bones* reappear briefly in *Sing, Unburied, Sing*, when Leonie spots them and thinks, "That girl so lucky. She has all her brothers" (197). Readers of the previous book know Esch to be anything but lucky; however, this focus on survival, at the very moment when the Stone family has returned home from their perilous journey, emphasizes the importance of maintaining the human community even when its physical walls have been washed away.

Crossing themes in this way demonstrates that novels representing intersectional identities like the ones discussed here yield multiple potentials for ongoing conversations and collaborations. The longer conversations staged in each chapter center around authors who identify as part of the same ethnic community, and who have a documented connection of influence from one to another. However, gender, class, and race dynamics combine in multiple ways beyond these samplings. Each of the novels discussed here has resonances with many others beyond the scope of this book. The readings here strive to weave a selection of texts together, and hopefully each will open new possibilities for further connections.

FROM FICTION TO ACTION AND BACK AGAIN

Finally, this is a book about how reading inspires more reading and more writing in turn, forging increasing awareness and understanding of intersectional identities too varied and complex for any one individual to experience. When students voice the familiar complaint that analysis "ruins" the pleasure of a text, I remind them that literary criticism deepens our joy in literature by expanding our understanding beyond what may be obvious to us, in our unique subject positions, the first time we open a book. Sandra Cisneros puts this most eloquently in her description of reading:

> I often remember where I was when meeting a book that sweeps me off my feet. I remember the moment and the intimate sensation of devouring a beloved text as distinctly as I recall the most sensual encounters of my life. Is it like this for everyone, or is it like this only for those who work with words? I want

to believe everyone falls in love with a book in much the same way one falls in love with a person, that one has an intimate, personal exchange, a mystical exchange as spiritual and charged as the figure eight meaning infinity. (*House of My Own* 117)

Cisneros' lush description may feel familiar to many lovers of literature, but she interrupts the emotional tone of her writing with an alliterative but mono-syllabic and choppy phrase, wondering if her experience only parallels that of "those who work with words." The phrase, almost evoking manual labor, sug-gests that someone so impacted by literature must also be someone compelled to forge more literature in turn. The reference to the "figure eight meaning infinity" at the end is an apt one to apply to this process: Cisneros reads, so she must write; other writers like the ones discussed here read Cisneros and must write in turn, and so on, infinitely.

Writing is, of course, one way of taking social action, but fiction's abil-ity to encourage our empathy for other people can move us to other forms of activism as well. Kingston, an activist herself, makes this point in an interview with Shelley Fisher Fishkin: "What we need to do is to be able to *imagine* the possibility of a playful, peaceful, nurturing, mothering man, and we need to imagine the possibilities of a powerful, nonviolent woman and the possibilities of harmonious communities—and if we can just *imagine* them, that would be the first step toward building them and becoming them" (783). Kingston expresses here a belief in the power of literature to create new ways of being. She specifically envisions how breaking gender roles could be a way to move towards "harmonious communities," and elaborates later in the interview: "We have to change human consciousness and that's a step towards changing the material world" (783). Transforming her readers, giving them more empathy towards others unlike them, can lead to lasting impacts for the oppressed. Fatima Mujcinovic agrees that Kingston's work has this potential: "in conditions of domination and oppression, literacy becomes an emerging act of consciousness, resistance, and liberation for the oppressed and marginalized" (111). As Mujcinovic argues, the increased accessibility such literature provides can pave the way for greater opportunities for social change. She adds that it can even give readers the "determination to continue expressing one's authentic voice and experiences and thus participating in the pursuit of social justice" (111). Although Mujcinovic does not focus on empathy as the key agent for this change, as I do, she argues convincingly that literature can move readers to positions of activism.

There is increasing scientific evidence to confirm this as well. In chapter one, I discussed some of the growing body of scientific research supporting the idea that reading fiction creates empathy. Further research demonstrates that fiction can move us from empathy to action. In 2020, researchers at the

University of Toronto studied the impact of reading fiction, in contrast to non-fiction, on decreasing the need for "cognitive closure" and thus allowing a greater capacity for open-mindedness and empathy. They found that fiction did indeed allow the participants in the study to "simulate other minds" and feel less "discomfort with ambiguity" (Djikic et al. 153). The authors explain that this occurs in part because when reading fiction, we don't need to defend our own standpoint; we can simply take on the perspective of someone very different from ourselves without feeling we have sacrificed our own. In this way we can achieve what Keats called "negative capability," or the capacity to dwell "in uncertainties, Mysteries, doubts, without any irritable reaching after fact & reason" (poetryfoundation.org). The researchers' conclusion connects negative capability derived from fiction to the potential to take action: "It is hoped that this experiment will stimulate further investigation into the potential of literature in opening closed minds, as well as give one a pause to think about the effects of current cut-backs of education in the arts and humanities" (Djikic et al. 153). Reading fiction creates more empathic citizens, which causes the scientific researchers to advocate for arts and humanities funding; more such funding might encourage future students to take action of their own.

Other research has looked more deeply into the connection between fiction and action. Dan R. Johnson, Professor of Cognitive and Behavioral Sciences at Washington and Lee, concludes that reading leads not only to greater empathy but also to "pro-social action." In a 2013 study he found that participants who felt "transported" by the story—able to visualize it clearly, interested in knowing more about the characters—were also more likely to act altruistically by picking up strategically dropped pens afterwards. The author concludes that "if children are encouraged to read fictional stories that include characters that elicit empathy and exhibit prosocial behavior, they may develop the same behavior" (154). Reading fiction, and reading it well, can help us help others. While retrieving pens may be but one small example, it seems plausible that a "micro-kindness" can prove as beneficial as micro-aggressions are known to be harmful. It is at least a place to begin: Minor pro-social actions have the potential to expand to ones of greater consequence.

Coming from a different perspective, culture and politics writer Alyssa Rosenberg writes about how the 2010 trend of listing "Ten Books" that influenced you begged the question of where that influence might lead. She shared her own story of how a childhood book inspired her to join a protest for financial aid at Yale: "The memory of a fictional flower-seller and the influence of his arrest was one of the things that helped me say yes when my friends needed one more person to make the sit-in successful. *The Pushcart War* was one of the books that pushed me, a terminal bookworm, out into the world, that made me not just think, but act." Not all influences are political, and she describes the impact of books on her romantic and personal identity formation as well; but I would argue that if reading can shape our human interactions and our character, it will lead many to public action. Understanding the interiority of others can and should lead us to shape a more inclusive society.

This book began many years ago, from many conversations with many different novels. Its current form began when I found myself immersed in a relatively unknown book by a new author, *Everything I Never Told You*. In that book, Ng quotes another book, which inspires by counterexample: Dale Carnegie's 1936 self-help book, *How to Win Friends and Influence People,* advises, "Remember that the people you are talking to are a hundred times more interested in themselves and their wants and problems than they are in you and your problems" (qtd. in Ng 180). According to Carnegie, self-interest is innate, and success requires that we lean into rather than contradict that fact. But Ng's novel persistently counterargues that such disregard for others can lead to neglect, trauma, or even death; her book undoes the previous book it cites.

Some eight year later, as I was revising this book, Celeste Ng published her third novel, *Our Missing Hearts*. If her first book whispered a retort to Carnegie's validation of self-interest, this one shouts it. Set in a dystopic near-future, the novel imagines a world very close to our own in which an economic crisis amplifies paranoia about China, "that perilous, perpetual yellow menace," to Red Scare levels of mass hysteria (161). Soon the government begins removing children from their parents if they express any "un-American" or pro-Chinese sympathies. In case we missed the news stories of immigrant children stolen from their mothers at the border and permanently "misplaced": "There was a long history of children taken, the pretexts different but the reasons the same. A most precious ransom, a cudgel over a parent's head. It was whatever the opposite of an anchor was: an attempt to uproot some otherness, something hated and feared. Some foreignness seen as an invasive weed, something to be eradicated" (238). Ng's book seems designed to incite contemporary readers to action, both through arguments like these and through the modeled actions of her characters.

The solution to Ng's dystopia comes through the writings of a woman of color whose words produce radical empathy in her readers. Margaret Miu pens a book of apolitical poems; a young Black woman finds it and protests the child abductions using one line: the titular "all our missing hearts." When she is murdered by police, the full poem goes viral. The subsequent resistance movement is orchestrated by librarians, bound in books at every turn. When Margaret must disappear to avoid her own child being stolen by the government, she leaves him a trail to find her—through books, of course. As a fugitive, Margaret organizes the great protest that will finally begin to crack the totalitarian government: She collects every story she can of every parent whose child has been abducted, and projects herself reading them through speakers hidden throughout Manhattan: "only one voice, but speaking the words of many" (293). It is not the individual details, but the collective remembrance that matters most: "None of the stories were important . . . all of the stories were unbearably important" (219). The protest works because everyone can empathize with the grief of these parents and the anguish of these children, and everyone can experience those emotions as their own. Ng describes individual reactions from those listening but also a collective response: "It was somehow speaking not just to them but with them, of them, that the stories it told, one after the other in a seemingly endless stream, were not someone else's but one larger story of which they, too, were a part" (296). While the book doesn't end with a full-blown coup, it shows the beginning of change in every person who hears these stories, remembers them, and passes them on.

Our Missing Hearts seems the natural conclusion to Ng's first two novels, carrying her themes of motherhood and responsibility into the public sphere. Appropriately, it moves out of the past, where her first two novels are set, and into the future. In her 2016 talk "Reflecting on Cultural Identity, Race, and Family," Celeste Ng succinctly states one of the central tenets of her work: "I really believe that the best fiction is an exercise in empathy, in imagining what it's like to be someone else" (10:05). The capacity to do so, her third novel suggests, may just be all that can save us from intolerance and despair. She concludes the talk with her greatest wish for the readers of her work: "I always hope that they'll close the book thinking about what they don't know about other people, and ways that they can bridge those gaps between other people and themselves" (10:32). This is certainly what her book, and all the others discussed here, did for me. I hope that when closing this book, readers will open others, and continue to learn more about all we have left to learn.

NOTES

1. For more on this topic, see Jean Wyatt, discussed in chapter one.

2. The neighborhood also has Italians who, in the World War II era of the book's setting, were not considered equal to Whites.

Appendix

Multicultural Book Club: More Books to Try If You Find One (Or a Genre) You Love

If you loved	Try	Because
The Woman Warrior (Kingston)	Beloved (Morrison)	Historical fiction, feminism, ghosts
	Dreaming in Cuban (Garcia)	Poetic intergenerational immigrant story
	Americanah (Adiche)	Africa to America feminist novel
Everything I Never Told You (Ng)	Buddah in the Attic (Otsuka)	Japanese internment; minimalist
	Unaccustomed Earth (Lahiri)	Beautiful, minimalist, focused on families
	Jazz (Morrison)	Elegiac Harlem Renaissance murder/romance
Song of Solomon (Morrison)	Black Boy (Wright)	Stunning lyrical autobiography
	Invisible Man (Ellison)	Classic introspection on Black identity
	Love Medicine (Erdrich)	Brilliant writing; emphasis on community
Sing, Unburied, Sing (Ward)	An American Marriage (Jones)	Impacts of the prison-industrial complex
	Ceremony (Silko)	Postwar trauma and healing
	A Burning (Majumdar)	Poverty and its many impacts in India
The House on Mango Street (Cisneros)	Claire of the Sea Light (Danticat)	Impressionistic Haitian childhood portrait

	Brown Girl Dreaming (Woodson)	Poetic young-adult *bildungsroman*
	Absolutely True Autobiography of a So-Called Indian (Alexie)	Race and poverty viewed by an engaging adolescent
Sabrina and Corina (Fajardo-Anstine)	*The Aguero Sisters* (Garcia)	Opposite/connected sisters, family
	Drinking Coffee Elsewhere (Packer)	Direct style; complex race/gender themes
	Brief Encounters with Che Guevara (Fountain)	Interconnected short stories of Haiti
Woman of Light (Fajardo-Anstine)	*The Poisonwood Bible* (Kingsolver)	Missionary family transformed in/by Africa
	Underground Railroad (Whitehead)	Strong female's struggles in alternate history
	In the Time of the Butterflies (Alvarez)	Dominican feminist historical fiction
Drama	*Pass Over* (Nwandu)	*Waiting for Godot* with racism
	Topdog/Underdog (Parks)	Black masculinity, brothers divided
	Angels in America (Kushner)	All the intersectionalities!
	At Night We Walk in Circles (Alarcon)	A play-within-a-novel about the play
	Tripmaster Monkey: His Fake Book (Kingston)	Also a play-within-a-novel; hilarious, po-modern
Short story collections	*Krik? Krak!* (Danticat)	Lovely Haitian story collection
	Toughest Indian in the World (Alexie)	Humorous Native American stories
	Bloodchild (Butler)	Delightfully bizarre sci-fi stories
	Interpreter of Maladies (Lahiri)	Beautiful Pulitzer-winning first collection
	What Is Not Yours Is Not Yours (Oyeymi)	Incredible magical realist stories
	The Refugees (Nguyen)	Complex Vietnamese-American stories
Memoir	*Reading Lolita in Tehran* (Nafisi)	Memoir/literary criticism/history
	Between the World and Me (Coates)	Father-to-son letter on black manhood
	Bad Indians (Miranda)	Heartbreaking family/tribal history
	Men We Reaped (Ward)	Told-in-reverse story of five men's tragic deaths
Graphic Novels	*Maus* (Speigelman)	Most famous activist graphic novel

	March trilogy (Lewis)	Autobiography of a Civil Rights icon
	Persepolis (Satrapi)	Excellent Iranian graphic novel (especially Book 1)
	Y: The Last Man (Vaughn)	Funny/smart feminist graphic novel series
	My Favorite Thing Is Monsters (Ferris)	Lesbian Holocaust anxiety murder mystery
Science Fiction	*Broken Earth Trilogy* (Jimison)	Riveting Black eco-feminist sci-fi
	Binti Trilogy (Okorafor)	Compelling feminist Afro-futurism
	Never Let Me Go (Ishiguro)	British boarding school . . . that isn't . . .
	Future Home of the Living God (Erdrich)	Native American Handmaid's Tale-ish
Poetry/mixed genre	*Citizen* (Rankine)	Incredible multimedia poetry collection
	In the Dreamhouse (Machado)	Post-modern lesbian domestic abuse autobiography
	The Poet X (Acevedo)	Young-adult autobiographical poetry novel
Intergenerational family sagas	*Love Medicine* (Erdrich)	Her first epic novel in a long saga
	Salt Houses (Alyan)	Intergenerational Palestinian family story
	White Teeth (Smith)	Epic, brilliant, insightful, funny
	Brief Wonderous Life of Oscar Wao (Diaz)	Dominican family drama plus nerd culture
	Almanac of the Dead (Silko)	Mexican/Indian epic; hilarious, audacious
Magical Realism	*100 Years of Solitude* (Garcia Marquez)	The gold standard, influencing everything
	The Moor's Last Sigh (Rushdie)	One of the best novels by a powerhouse novelist
	Exit West (Hamid)	Magical doors open borders everywhere
	So Far From God (Castillo)	The magical disintegration of a family of women
Stories of mixed races/cultures	*The Vanishing Half* (Bennett)	Twin sisters passing in different worlds
	Caucasia (Senna)	Sisters passing in a family divided
	Loving Day (Johnson)	Contemporary (funny) mixed race novel
	Mona in the Promised Land (Jen)	Chinese/Jewish, and funny

Appendix

Multicultural queer fiction	The Ministry of Utmost Happiness (Roy)	India's third gender normalized
	Black Leopard, Red Wolf (James)	Powerful, surreal African fantasy
	On Earth We're Briefly Gorgeous (Vuong)	Lyrical, beautiful, just start crying now
	Kiss of the Spider Women (Puig)	Postmodern Argentine love story in prison

Acknowledgments

My gratitude to Yale University, my first soul mother; New York University, where my mother and I both found love; and Regis University, my heart's home. I am especially thankful to Regis for multiple travel grants at conferences where I presented this work, and for honoring me as the Faculty Lecturer of the Year for 2019–2020, giving me both time and inspiration to write much of this. Thank you to all my teachers, including Tom Rice and Jay Grenawalt; Leslie Brisman; Cyrus Patell and Elizabeth McHenry; and especially Andrea Watson, who helped me see writing as both a joy and a profession. Thank you to all my students, from Graland to N.Y.U. to Regis, for inspiring me every day. Extra thanks to my wonderful research assistants, Isabella Dino and Raina Miyake, who graciously provided exactly the help I needed, exactly when I needed it.

I am deeply grateful to all of my phenomenal colleagues at Regis. I give extra honors to my Honors friends: Tom Howe, who looks for the big questions while I'm immersed in the details; Cath Kleier, an exuberant friend and an intrepid adventurer; and Amy Schreier, a paragon for how to work efficiently, laugh frequently, and converse endlessly. As always, my respect, admiration, and love go out to my English department family: Alyse Knorr and Kate Partridge, both incredible poetesses, generous friends, and my other favorite academic couple; Nick Myklebust, gifted linguist and friend to the lagomorphs; and Mark Bruhn, whom we lost too soon but whose mark on Regis is undying. And extra thanks to my two beloved mentors in empathic literary pedagogy, whose words, books, and lives inspire mine: David Hicks, for whom I would make chicken parmigiana any time, and the incomparable Daryl Palmer, my dream-symbol for care, compassion, and courage.

My lifelong friends have given me incalculable support. My deepest gratitude to Lisa Kron and Jamie Cordial for growing up with me and sharing all our secrets from nerd-camp crushes to the birth of our children and everything in between; to Christine Graham, Allison Hall, Emily Kim, and Emily Hinsdale for helping me find the end of the rainbow and never stop looking for it again; to Kelly Kelly, Helen Bailey, Mary Sheridan, and Gabriella Serruya for making New Haven a haven, and Yale a home; and to Mike and Mira Killmeyer, Jennifer Engelmann, and Shawn Harris for dinner party camaraderie at once raucous, ridiculous, and real. And all the thanks to my virtual-sister-for-life, Anne Krendl, for sharing her family and nearly everything else with me since sixth grade, and because nothing makes sense until we talk about it for hours. As her (our) mother foretold, we never stop co-writing the playscript of our lives.

Finally, I am grateful every day for having been raised in a family who loves literature and learning. Thanks to my hyper-literate Jersey Jew clan who make daily events into holidays and holidays into extravaganzas, especially my superwomen heroes: Aunt Diane, legendary storyteller and impromptu comedian; Julie Dobrow, angelic singer and working-mom boss; Ilyse ("Lisi") Dobrow, writer and listener extraordinaire who created entire childhood fantasy worlds with me and makes compassion an art form; and Heather Stein, survivor and caretaker, who makes Passover dinners infinitely more fun.

Thanks to my kindhearted brother, Scott Narcisi. You are My Hometown. To his beloved family of strong women, Rachael, Eliana, and Makenzie Narcisi: mahalo for endless meals and theatricals, adventures and laughter.

Thanks to my brilliant father, who gave me his passion for learning, endless curiosity, a fighting spirit, and unconditional love. Who else would be by my side from furry bedtime stories to weeping at Pavarotti?

Thanks to my mother, my soulmate, Permafriend, and first teacher, who wove stories with me of romance, mystery, and the occasional Soviet spy; whose whimsical heart gave me a magical childhood; who raised me on homemade cookies and homegrown activism; who has always believed I should write my own stories, and who has listened to every single one I've ever told.

Thanks to my beloved sons, Quentin and Beckett, for letting me read and tell them a million stories, and for sharing their own with me; for making me laugh, for filling me with pride, and for giving me hope for the future.

And thanks to my husband, Scott Dimovitz, my favorite author and the exemplary editor who read and helped hone every word of this book; my fellow life-long learner and fellow traveler, who had my heart when he made a book of our love letters out of duct tape, when he invited me to Dublin for Bloomsday, when he proposed to me with a bookshelf, and every day since.

Works Cited

Adichie, Chimamanda Ngozi. "The Danger of a Single Story." TED Talk, 2009. https://www.ted.com/talks/chimamanda_adichie_the_danger_of_a_single_story?language=en.

Athena, Emma. "Can 'Woman of Light' Rewrite the Western Mythology?" *Boulder Weekly*, June 2, 2022.

Awkward, Michael. "'Unruly and Let Loose': Myth, Ideology, and Gender in *Song of Solomon*." In *Toni Morrison's Song of Solomon: A Casebook*, edited by Jan Furman (Oxford University Press, 2003).

Baldwin, James. "Alas, Poor Richard." *Nobody Knows My Name: More Notes of a Native Son*, (Delta, 1961, 1962), 181–215.

———. "East River, Downtown: Postscript to a Letter from Harlem." *Nobody Knows My Name: More Notes of a Native Son* (Delta, 1961, 1962), 72–82.

———. "Fifth Avenue, Uptown: A Letter From Harlem." *Nobody Knows My Name: More Notes of a Native Son* (Delta, 1961, 1962), 56–71.

Blake, William. "London." https://www.poetryfoundation.org/poems/43673/london-56d222777e969.

Burcar, Lilijana. "Shortcomings and Limitations of Identity Politics and Intersectionality in Sandra Cisneros's *The House on Mango Street.*" *Acta Neophilologica* 51, no. 1–2 (2018), 25–38.

Calloway, Catherine. "Parchman, Imprisonment, and Liminality in Jesmyn Ward's *Sing, Unburied, Sing*." *The Philological Review* 45, no. 2 (2019), 55–82.

Chase, Greg. "Of Trips Taken and Time Served: How Ward's *Sing, Unburied, Sing* Grapples with Faulkner's Ghosts." *African American Review* 53, no. 3 (Fall 2020), 201–16.

Cheney, Alexandra. "Toni Morrison, Maxine Hong Kingston and Leslie Marmon Silko Remember China." *The Wall Street Journal*, February 1, 2011. https://www.wsj.com/articles/BL-SEB-61806.

Cheung, King-Kok. *Articulate Silences: Hisaye Yamamoto, Maxine Hong Kingston, Joy Kogawa* (Cornell University Press, 1993).

Chin, Frank. "Confessions of a Chinatown Cowboy." *Bulletproof Buddhists and Other Essays*, (University of Hawaii Press, 1998), 65–110.

Chin, Frank, Jeffery Paul Chan, Lawson Fusao Inada, and Shawn Wong, eds. *Aiiieeeee!: An Anthology of Asian-American Writers* (Mentor, 1974, 1991).

Chin, Marilyn. "Writing the Other: A Conversation with Maxine Hong Kingston." *Conversations with Maxine Hong Kingston*, edited by Paul Skenazy and Tera Martin (University Press of Mississippi, 1998), 86–103. https://search-ebscohost-com.dml.regis.edu/login.aspx?direct=true&db=mzh&AN=1998055297&site=ehost-live&scope=site.

Cisneros, Sandra. "Chocolate and Donuts." *A House of My Own: Stories from My Life* (Vintage International, 2016), 331–36.

———. "Do You Know Me?: I Wrote *The House on Mango Street*." *The Americas Review* 15, no.1 (Spring 1987) 77–79.

———. "Ghosts and Voices: Writing from Obsession." *The Americas Review* 15, no. 1 (Spring 1987), 69–73.

———. *The House on Mango Street* (Vintage International, 1984, 1988).

———. "*The House on Mango Street*'s Tenth Birthday." *A House of My Own: Stories from My Life* (Vintage International, 2016), 124–31.

———. "Infinito Botánica." *A House of My Own: Stories from My Life* (Vintage International, 2016), 215–18.

———. "On the Solitary Fate of Being Mexican, Female, Wicked and Thirty-three." Interview by Pilar E. Rodríguez-Aranda. *The Americas Review* 18, no.1 (1990), 64–80.

———. "Living as a Writer: Choice and Circumstance." *Revista Mujeres* 3, no. 2 (June 1986) 68–72.

———. "*Mi Casa es Su Casa*." *A House of My Own: Stories from My Life* (Vintage International, 2016), 170–76.

———. "My Purple House: Color Is a Language and a History," *San Antonio Express News*, August 31, 1997.

———. "Notes to a Young(er) Writer," *The Americas Review* 15, no. 1 (Spring 1987), 74–77.

———. *¡Que Vivan Los Colores!*. *A House of My Own: Stories from My Life* (Vintage International, 2016), 170–76.

———. "Resurrections." *A House of My Own: Stories from My Life* (Vintage International, 2016), 298–302.

———. "*Tenemos* Layaway, Or, How I Became an Art Collector." *A House of My Own: Stories from My Life* (Vintage International, 2016), 177–90.

———. "To Seville, with Love." *A House of My Own: Stories from My Life* (Vintage International, 2016), 226–34.

———. *Woman Hollering Creek* (Vintage, 1991).

Clance, Pauline and Suzanne Imes. "The Imposter Phenomenon in High Achieving Women: Dynamics and Therapeutic Intervention." *Psychotherapy: Theory, Research & Practice* 15, no. 3 (1978), 241–47. https://doi.org/10.1037/h0086006.

Coates, Ta-Nehisi. *Between the World and Me* (Spiegel and Grau, 2015).

Collins, Patricia Hill. *Black Feminist Thought: Knowledge, Consciousness, and the Politics of Empowerment* (Routledge, 2022).

Crenshaw, Kimberlé. "Mapping the Margins: Intersectionality, Identity Politics, and Violence Against Women of Color," *Stanford Law Review* 43, no. 6 (1991), 1241, https://doi.org/10.2307/1229039.

Davis, Olga Idriss. "The Door of No Return: Reclaiming the Past Through the Rhetoric of Pilgrimage," *The Western Journal of Black Studies* 21, no. 3 (1997), 156–61.

Dib, Nicole. "Haunted Roadscapes in Jesmyn Ward's *Sing, Unburied, Sing.*" *MELUS: The Journal of the Society for the Study of the Multi-Ethnic Literature of the United States* 45, no. 2 (June 2020), 134–53.

Dillard, Annie. *For the Time Being* (Vintage, 2000).

Dillender, Kirsten. "Land and Pessimistic Futures in Contemporary African American Speculative Fiction," *Extrapolation* 61, no. 1 (March 2020), 131.

Djikic, Maja, Keith Oatley, and Mihnea Moldoveanu. "Opening the Closed Mind: The Effect of Exposure to Literature on the Need for Closure," *Creativity Research Journal* 25, no. 2 (April 2013), 149–54. https://doi-org.dml.regis.edu/10.1080/10400419.2013.783735.

Doyle, Jacqueline. "More Room of Her Own: Sandra Cisneros's *The House on Mango Street,*" *MELUS* 19, no. 4 (1994), 5–35.

Dubek, Laura. "'Pass It On!': Legacy and the Freedom Struggle in Toni Morrison's *Song of Solomon,*" *The Southern Quarterly: A Journal of the Arts in the South* 52, no. 2 (2015), 90–109.

Duncan, Patti L. "The Uses of Silence: Notes on the Will to Unsay." In *Women of Color: Defining the Issues, Hearing the Voices*, edited by Diane Long Hoeveler and Janet K. Boles (Greenwood Press, 2001).

Dwyer, June. "Ethnic Home Improvement: Gentrifying the Ghetto, Spicing Up the Suburbs," *ISLE: Interdisciplinary Studies in Literature and Environment* 14, no. 2 (2007), 165–82.

Eliot, T.S. "The Waste Land." https://www.poetryfoundation.org/poems/47311/the-waste-land.

Ellison, Ralph. *Invisible Man* (Vintage International, 1947, 1995).

Fajardo-Anstine, Kali. "Heritage and Home." Interview by Teague Bohlen, *Westword*, April 3, 2019.

———. "On the 32." Keynote Address, Regis University, April 7, 2021.

———. *Sabrina and Corina* (Random House, 2019).

———. *Woman of Light* (One World, 2022).

Fanon, Frantz. *Black Skin, White Masks* (Grove Press, 1967).

Faulkner, William. *Absalom, Absalom!* (Vintage International, 1936, 1990).

———. Address upon Receiving the Nobel Prize for Literature. *The Portable Faulkner*, edited by Malcolm Cowley (Penguin, 1946, 1977).

———. *As I Lay Dying* (Vintage International, 1930, 1990).

———. *Light in August* (Vintage International, 1932, 1990).

———. *The Sound and the Fury*, edited by David Minter (Norton Critical Edition, 1929, 1994).

Fishkin, Shelley Fisher. "Interview with Maxine Hong Kingston," *American Literary History* 3, no. 4 (1991), 782–91. https://doi-org.dml.regis.edu/10.1093/alh/3.4.782

Frazer, Elizabeth and Nicola Lacey. *A Feminist Critique of the Liberal-Communitarian Debate* (University of Toronto Press, 1993).

Freedman, Eden Wales. *Reading Testimony, Witnessing Trauma: Confronting Race, Gender, and Violence in American Literature* (University Press of Mississippi, 2020).

Frydman, Jason. "Upward Mobility as a Neurotic Condition in Sandra Cisneros' *The House on Mango Street*," *Exit 9: The Rutgers Journal of Comparative Literature* 8 (2007), 15–23.

Ganz, Robin. "Sandra Cisneros: Border Crossings and Beyond," *MELUS, The Society for the Study of the Multi-Ethnic Literature of the United States* 19, no. 1 (Spring 1994), 19–29.

García-Avello, Macarena. "Beyond the Latina Boom: New Directions within the Field of U.S. Latina Literature," *ATLANTIS: Journal of the Spanish Association of Anglo-American Studies* 41, no.1 (2019), 69–87.

Gasztold, Brygida. "Between the Need to Fit in and the Desire to Stand Out: Race, Gender, and Sexuality in Celeste Ng's *Everything I Never Told You*," In *Disrespected Neighbo(u)Rs: Cultural Stereotypes in Literature and Film*, edited by Caroline Rosenthal et al. (Cambridge Scholars Publishing, 2018), 62–78.

Gee, Alison Singh. "Novelist Celeste Ng on Her New Book, Rules To Be Broken, and Why She Isn't Set on Writing the Great Chinese-American Novel," *South China Morning Post,* October 20, 2017, https://www.scmp.com/culture/books/article /2115916/novelist-celeste-ng-her-new-book-rules-be-broken-and-why-she-isnt-set.

Gersen, Jeannie Suk. "At Trial, Harvard's Asian Problem and a Preference for White Students from 'Sparse Country,'" *The New Yorker,* October 23, 2018.

Gettleman, Jeffrey. "The Peculiar Position of India's Third Gender," *The New York Times*, February 17, 2018. https://www.nytimes.com/2018/02/17/style/india-third -gender-hijras-transgender.html.

Givens, Terri. *Radical Empathy: Finding a Path to Bridging Racial Divides* (Policy Press, 2021).

Gonzalez, Susan. "In Class Day Address, Clinton Encourages Students to Keep up Their Fight," *Yale News,* May 22, 2018, https://news.yale.edu/2018/05/21/class -day-address-clinton-encourages-students-keep-their-fight.

Griffin, Farah Jasmine. *Read Until You Understand: The Profound Wisdom of Black Life and Literature* (W.W. Norton & Co., 2021).

Hall, Eilidh AB. *Negotiating Feminisms: Sandra Cisneros and Ana Castillo's Intergenerational Women* (Palgrave Macmillan, 2021).

Hancock, Ange-Marie. *Intersectionality: An Intellectual History* (Oxford University Press, 2016).

Hartman, Saidiya. "Innocent Amusements," *Scenes of Subjection: Terror, Slavery, and Self-Making in Nineteenth Century America* (Oxford University Press, 1997).

Hartnell, Anna. "When Cars Become Churches: Jesmyn Ward's Disenchanted America," *Cambridge Core,* November 2013.

Hedges, Elaine and Shelley Fisher Fishkin, eds. *Listening to Silences: New Essays in Feminist Criticism* (Oxford University Press, 1994).

Hernandez, Elizabeth. "This Highly Anticipated New Book Is Set in 1930s Denver, a City on the Brink of Change," *The Denver Post*, June 13, 2022.

———. ""Where We Come from Is Art': Denver's Gentrifying Northside Captured Through the Lens and Poetry of Its Latino Youth," *The Denver Post*, December 19, 2021.

Holt, Eliott. "The Return of Omniscience," *New York Times Book Review*, September 8, 2016, https://www.nytimes.com/2016/09/11/books/review/the-return-of-omniscience.html.

Islas, Arturo, and Marilyn Yalom. "Interview with Maxine Hong Kingston." In *Conversations with Maxine Hong Kingston*, edited by Paul Skenazy and Tera Martin (University Press of Mississippi, 1998).

Iwata, Edward. "Is It a Clash Over Writing . . . ," *The Los Angeles Times*. June 24, 1990. https://www.latimes.com/archives/la-xpm-1990-06-24-vw-1117-story.html.

Johnson, Dan R. "Transportation into a Story Increases Empathy, Prosocial Behavior, and Perceptual Bias Toward Fearful Expressions," *Personality and Individual Differences* 52, no. 2 (January 2012), 150–55. https://doi-org.dml.regis.edu/10.1016/j.paid.2011.10.005.

Jordan, Judith V., Schwartz, Harriet L., "Radical Empathy in Teaching." *New Directions for Teaching & Learning* 2018, no. 153 (Spring 2018).

Keats, John. "On Negative Capability: Letter to George and Tom Keats," December 22, 1818. https://www.poetryfoundation.org/articles/69384/selections-from-keatss-letters.

Keen, Suzanne. "A Theory of Narrative Empathy," *Narrative* 14, no. 3 (2006), 207–36.

Kingston, Maxine Hong. "A Letter in Response to Lara Narcisi," *Connotations* 13, no. 1–2 (January 2003), 179.

———. *China Men* (Vintage International, 1977, 1989).

———. "Coming Home." *Conversations with Maxine Hong Kingston*, edited by Paul Skenazy and Tera Martin (University Press of Mississippi, 1998).

———. "Cultural Mis-readings by American Reviewers," *Asian and Western Writers in Dialogue: New Cultural Identities*, edited by Guy Amirthanayagam (Macmillan, 1982), 55–57.

———. "I Can Write My Shadow." Interview by Alexis Cheung, *Los Angeles Review of Books*, December 22, 2016, https://lareviewofbooks.org/article/can-write-shadow-alexis-cheung-interviews-maxine-hong-kingston/.

———. "Special Eyes: The Chinese-American World of Maxine Hong Kingston." Interview by Angels Carabí, *Atlantis* 10. no. 1–2 (1988).

———. *Tripmaster Monkey: His Fake Book* (Vintage International, 1987, 1990).

———. *The Woman Warrior* (Vintage Books, 1976, 1989).

Kristeva, Julia, *Desire in Language: A Semiotic Approach to Literature and Art*, edited by Leon S. Roudiez, translated by Thomas Gora, Alice Jardine, and Leon S. Roudiez. (Columbia University Press, 1980).

Krumholz, Linda. "Dead Teachers: Rituals of Manhood and Rituals of Reading in *Song of Solomon*." In *Toni Morrison's Song of Solomon: A Casebook*, edited by Jan Furman (Oxford University Press, 2003).

Lamy, Nicole. "Celeste Ng Is More Than a Novelist," *The New York Times*, December 20, 2018, https://www.nytimes.com/2018/12/20/books/celeste-ng-everything-i -never-told-you-little-fires-everwhere.html.

Launius, Christie, and Holly Hassel. *Threshold Concepts in Women's and Gender Studies: Ways of Seeing, Thinking, and Knowing* (Routledge, 2022).

Lee, Catherine Carr. "The South in Toni Morrison's *Song of Solomon*: Initiation, Healing, and Home." In *Toni Morrison's Song of Solomon: A Casebook*, edited by Jan Furman (Oxford University Press, 2003).

Lee, Kang, Victoria Talwar, Anjanie McCarthy, Ilana Ross, Angela Evans, and Cindy Arruda. "Can Classic Moral Stories Promote Honesty in Children?" *Psychological Science* 25, no. 8 (2014), 1630–36. https://ggsc.berkeley.edu/images/uploads/Lee _et_al_2014_Can_Classic_Moral_Stories_Promote_Honesty_in_Children.pdf.

Ling, Jinqui, "Identity Crisis and Gender Politics: Reappropriating Asian American Masculinity." In *An Interethnic Companion to Asian American Literature*, edited by King-Kok Cheung (Cambridge University Press, 1997), 312–37.

Lorde, Audre. "The Transformation of Silence into Language and Action." In *Sister Outsider: Essays and Speeches* (Crossing Press, 2007), 40–44.

Lowinsky, Naomi. *The Motherline: Every Woman's Journey to Find Her Female Roots* (Fisher King Press, 1992, 2009).

Luna, Maria V. "Kali Fajardo-Anstine's Latinx Vision of the American West," *Electric Literature*, April 23, 2019.

Mayberry, Susan Neal. *Can't I Love What I Criticize?: The Masculine in Morrison* (University of Georgia Press, 2007).

Minh-ha, Trinh T. "Not You/Like You: Post-Colonial Women and the Interlocking Questions of Identity and Difference." Center for Cultural Studies, https:// culturalstudies.ucsc.edu/inscriptions/volume-34/trinh-t-minh-ha/.

———. *Woman, Native, Other: Writing Postcoloniality and Feminism* (Indiana University Press, 1989).

Moraga, Cherríe. "Catching Fire." In *This Bridge Called My Back: Writings of Radical Women of Color*, edited by Cherríe Moraga and Gloria Anzaldúa, fourth edition (State University of New York Press, 2015), xv–xxv.

———. "La Güera," *This Bridge Called My Back: Writings of Radical Women of Color*, fourth edition, edited by Cherríe Moraga and Gloria Anzaldúa (SUNY Press, 2015), 22–29.

Morrison, Toni. *Beloved* (Vintage International, 1987, 2004).

———. *The Bluest Eye* (Penguin, 1970, 1994).

———. *Jazz* (Plume, 1992, 1993).

———. "Rootedness: The Ancestor as Foundation." In *Black Women Writers (1950–1980): A Critical Evaluation*, edited by Mari Evans (Anchor-Doubleday, 1984), 339–45.

———. *Song of Solomon* (Vintage International, 1977, 2004).

———. "Toni Morrison: Segregation and Racism in Lorain, Ohio," April 20, 2010. https://www.youtube.com/watch?v=xeoFyiMvQQQ

————. "Unspeakable Things Unspoken: The Afro-American Presence in American Literature." In *The Source of Self-Regard: Selected Essays, Speeches, and Mediations* (Knopf, 2019).

Mujcinovic, Fatima. "Self-Expression and World-Expression: Critical Multicultural Literacy in Maxine Hong Kingston and Sandra Cisneros." *CEA Critic: An Official Journal of the College English Association* 76, no. 1 (March 2014), 98–113.

Murray, Rolland. "The Long Strut: *Song of Solomon* and the Emancipatory Limits of Black Patriarchy." *Callaloo* 22, no. 1 (1999), 121–33.

Myer, Chingyen Yang. "Breaking Silences: Telling Asian American Female Subversive Stories in Maxine Hong Kingston's *The Woman Warrior* and Fae Myenne Ng's *Bone*," *Asiatic: IIUM Journal of English Language and Literature* 11, no. 1 (June 2017), 211–28.

Nafisi, Azar. *Reading Lolita in Tehran* (Random House, 2004).

National Community Reinvestment Coalition, NCRC.org, June 2020.

Ng, Audrey. "Written by the Body: Evolutions of Embodiment in Maxine Hong Kingston's *The Woman Warrior* and *I Love a Broad Margin to My Life*," *MELUS* 44, no. 3 (2019), 155–74. https://doi-org.dml.regis.edu/10.1093/melus/mlz021.

Ng, Celeste. @pronounced_ing. "THE WOMAN WARRIOR, by Maxine Hong Kingston. A classic, for a reason. #BookLoversDay." *Twitter*, August 9, 2017, 9:37 a.m., https://twitter.com/pronounced_ing/status/895323262443413504.

————. "Celeste Ng: 'It's a Novel about Race, and Class and Privilege,'" *The Guardian*, by Paul Laity. November 4, 2017, https://www.theguardian.com/books/2017/nov/04/celeste-ng-interview-little-fires-everywhere.

————. *Everything I Never Told You* (Penguin, 2014).

————. "First Fiction 2014," *Poets & Writers,* by Ru Freeman. July/August 2014, pp. 46–47.

————. "Kirkus TV Interview with Bestselling Author Celeste Ng," December 15, 2014, https://www.youtube.com/watch?v=iNmRgZuG6kw.

————. *Little Fires Everywhere* (Penguin Press, 2017).

————. *Our Missing Hearts* (Penguin, 2022).

————. "Reflecting on Cultural Identity, Race, and Family." Conference on the First-Year Experience, February 20–23, 2016, Orlando, FL. https://www.youtube.com/watch?v=kVuEL_0YGkE.

————. "'There Aren't a Lot of You Out There': What? Let's Fix our Female Asian-American Writer Blind Spot Now." *Salon*, January 1, 2015, https://www.salon.com/2015/01/01/there_arent_a_lot_of_you_out_there_what_lets_fix_our_female_asian_american_writer_blind_spot_now/.

————. "Why I Don't Want to Be the Next Amy Tan," *Huffington Post,* March 18, 2010, https://www.huffpost.com/entry/why-i-dont-want-to-be-the_b_342340.

Ng, Fae Mynne. *Bone* (Hachette, 1993, 2014).

Nye, Naomi Shihab. "Lights in the Windows," *The Alan Review* 22, no. 3 (Spring 1995).

Olsen, Tillie. *Silences* (Delacorte Press/Seymour Lawrence, 1978).

Oshinsky, David. *"Worse Than Slavery": Parchman Farm and the Ordeal of Jim Crow Justice* (Free Press Paperbacks, 1997).

Parikh, Crystal. "Dissolution." *The Cambridge Companion to Twenty-First-Century American Fiction*, edited by Joshua Miller (Cambridge University Press, 2021), 234–50.

Parrott, Jill M. "Power and Discourse: Silence as Rhetorical Choice in Maxine Hong Kingston's *The Woman Warrior,*" *Rhetorica: A Journal of the History of Rhetoric* 30, no. 4 (2012), 375–91.

Poorman, Elisabeth. "Why Does America Still Have So Few Female Doctors?" *The Guardian,* January 14, 2018, https://www.theguardian.com/commentisfree/2018/jan/14/why-are-there-still-so-few-female-doctors.

Prince, Valerie Sweeney. *Burnin' Down the House: Home in African American Literature* (Columbia University Press, 2005).

Quintana, Alvina. "Borders Be Damned: Creolizing Literary Relations," *Cultural Studies* 13, no. 2, 358–66.

Rankine, Claudia. *Citizen: An American Lyric* (Graywolf Press, 2014).

Rich, Adrienne. "It Is the Lesbian in Us . . . " In *On Lies, Secrets, and Silence: Selected Prose, 1966–1978* (Norton, 1979), 199–202.

Richardson, Jason, Bruce Mitchell and Jad Edlebi. "Gentrification and Disinvestment 2020." *National Community Reinvestment Coalition*, NCRC.org, June 2020.

Rosenberg, Alyssa. "When Books Inspire Action," *The Atlantic,* March 29, 2010. https://www.theatlantic.com/entertainment/archive/2010/03/when-books-inspire -action/38149/.

Roy, Arundhati. *The Ministry of Utmost Happiness* (Vintage, 2017, 2018).

Sae-Saue, Jayson T. Gonzales, "The Inter-Ethnic Return: Racial and Cultural Multiplicity in Foundational Asian American and Chicana/o Literatures," *Comparative American Studies: An International Journal* 8, no. 4 (December 2010), 267–82.

Sagel, Jim. "PW Interviews: Sandra Cisneros," *Publishers Weekly,* March 29, 1991, pp. 74–75.

Sanneh, Kelefa. "Is Gentrification Really a Problem?" *The New Yorker*, July 4, 2016.

Serpell, Namwali. "On Toni Morrison and Black Difficulty," *Slate*, March 26, 2019, https://slate.com/culture/2019/03/toni-morrison-difficulty-black-women.html.

Shorris, Earl. "On the Uses of a Liberal Education: II. As a Weapon in the Hands of the Restless Poor," *Harpers*, September 1997. https://harpers.org/archive/1997/09/ ii-as-a-weapon-in-the-hands-of-the-restless-poor/.

Spice, Byron. "Reading Harry Potter: Carnegie Mellon Researchers Identify Brain Regions That Encode Words, Grammar, Character Development," *Carnegie Mellon University News*, November 26, 2014. https://www.cmu.edu/news/stories /archives/2014/november/november26_computationalreadingmodel.html#:~:text =Bit%20by%20bit%2C%20the%20algorithm,flying%20lesson%2C%22%20she %20noted.

Stepto, Robert. *A Home Elsewhere: Reading African American Classics in the Age of Obama* (Harvard University Press, 2010).

Stewart, Morgan Keith. "Deconstructing the Rose Metaphor and Cultivating Trees of Rebellion in Sandra Cisneros's *The House on Mango Street.*" *Latin American Literary Review* 47, no. 93 (2020), 37–48.

Taylor-Guthrie, Danille. *Toni Morrison: Conversations* (University Press of Mississippi, 2008).

Thorsteinson, Katherine. "From Escape to Ascension: The Effects of Aviation Technology on the Flying African Myth," *Criticism: A Quarterly for Literature and the Arts* 57, no. 2 (2015), 259–81.

Tokarczyk, Michelle M. *Class Definitions: On the Lives and Writings of Maxine Hong Kingston, Sandra Cisneros, and Dorothy Allison* (Susquehanna University Press, 2008).

Torres, Hector A. *Conversations with Contemporary Chicano and Chicana Writers* (University of New Mexico Press, 2007).

Turner, Rory. "Critical Radical Empathy and Cultural Sustainability." *Cultural Sustainabilities: Music, Media, Language, Advocacy*, edited by Timothy J. Cooley and Jeff Todd Titon (University of Illinois Press, 2019), 32–42. https://search-ebscohost-com.dml.regis.edu/login.aspx?direct=true&db=mzh&AN=202017976085&site=ehost-live&scope=site.

Tyre, Peg. "The Writing Revolution," *The Atlantic*, May 3, 2018, https://www.theatlantic.com/magazine/archive/2012/10/the-writing-revolution/309090/.

Ward, Jesmyn. "I Was Wandering. Toni Morrison Found Me," *New York Times*, August 9, 2019, https://www.nytimes.com/2019/08/09/opinion/sunday/i-was-wandering-toni-morrison-found-me.html.

———. *Men We Reaped* (Bloomsbury, 2013, 2014).

———. *Sing, Unburied, Sing* (Scribner, 2017).

———. *Salvage the Bones* (Scribner, 2011, 2012).

Wehbe, Leila, Brian Murphy, Partha Talukdar, Alona Fyshe, Aaditya Ramdas, and Tom Mitchell. "Simultaneously Uncovering the Patterns of Brain Regions Involved in Different Story Reading Subprocesses," *PLOS ONE, Public Library of Science,* 2014, https://doi.org/10.1371/journal.pone.0112575

Whitman, Walt. "Song of Myself." https://www.poetryfoundation.org/poems/45477/song-of-myself-1892-version.

Woolf, Virginia. *A Room of One's Own* (Harcourt, 1929, 1989).

———. "How Should One Read a Book?" *The Yale Review* 89, no. 1 (2001), 41–52, https://doi.org/10.1111/0044-0124.00468.

Wu, Diane. "The Veritas Is Out There," *This American Life,* episode 663, December 7, 2018. https://www.thisamericanlife.org/663/transcript.

Wyatt, Jean. *Risking Difference: Identification, Race, and Community in Contemporary Fiction and Feminism* (SUNY Press, 2002).

Yamada, Mitsuye. "Invisibility Is an Unnatural Disaster: Reflections of an Asian American Woman," *This Bridge Called My Back: Writings of Radical Women of Color*, fourth edition, edited by Cherríe Moraga and Gloria Anzaldúa (SUNY Press, 2015), 30–35.

Zou, Linda and Sapna Cheryan, "Diversifying Neighborhoods and Schools Engender Perceptions of Foreign Cultural Threat Among White Americans," *Journal of Experimental Psychology: General*, October 25, 2021.

Zou, Linda. "White Flight May Still Enforce Segregation." Interview with the American Psychological Association, October 25, 2021. https://www.apa.org/news/press/releases/2021/10/white-flight-segregation.

Index

About the Author

Dr. Lara Narcisi is professor of English and associate director of Honors at Regis University in Denver, Colorado. She teaches and writes about twentieth- to twenty-first-century American literature, particularly in the fields of race and gender studies. She holds degrees in English from Yale and New York University. Her essays appear in journals such as *MELUS* and *JMMLA*, and her book chapters appear in such collections as *American Indians and Popular Culture*, *Neo-Passing: Performing Identity After Jim Crow*, and *Jesmyn Ward: New Critical Essays*. She was Regis University's 2019–2020 Faculty Lecturer of the Year.

9 781666 921502